Accounting Classics Series

Publication of this Classic was made possible
by a grant from Arthur Andersen & Co.

Suggestions of titles to be included
in the Series are solicited and should be
addressed to the Editor

Accounting Publications of Scholars Book Co.

Robert R. Sterling, Editor

Sidney S. Alexander et al., *Five Monographs on Business Income*
Frank Sewell Bray, *The Accounting Mission*
F. Sewell Bray, *The Interpreation of Accounts*
Raymond J. Chambers, *Accounting, Evaluation and Economic Behavior*
Arthur Lowes Dickinson, *Accounting Practice and Procedure*
Edgar O. Edwards, Philip W. Bell, and L. Todd Johnson, *Accounting for Economic Events*
John B. Geijsbeek, *Ancient Double-Entry Bookkeeping*
Henry Rand Hatfield, *Accounting: Its Principles and Problems*
Bishop Carleton Hunt (Editor), *George Oliver May: Twenty-Five Years of Accounting Responsibility*
Yuji Ijiri, *The Foundations of Accounting Measurement*
Kenneth MacNeal, *Truth in Accounting*
Richard Mattessich, *Accounting and Analytical Methods*
George O. May, *Financial Accounting*
Paul D. Montagna, *Certified Public Accounting: A Sociological View of a Profession in Change*
William Andrew Paton, *Accounting Theory*
William Z. Ripley, *Main Street and Wall Street*
Charles W. Schandl, *Theory of Auditing*
DR Scott, *The Cultural Significance of Accounts*
Herbert A. Simon et al., *Centralization vs. Decentralization in Organizing the Controller's Department*
Charles E. Sprague, *The Philosophy of Accounts*
George J. Staubus, *Making Accounting Decisions*
George J. Staubus, *A Theory of Accounting to Investors*
Robert R. Sterling, *Theory of the Measurement of Enterprise Income*
Robert R. Sterling (Editor), *Asset Valuation and Income Determination*
Robert R. Sterling (Editor), *Institutional Issues in Public Accounting*
Robert R. Sterling (Editor), *Research Methodology in Accounting*
Robert R. Sterling and William F. Bentz (Editors), *Accounting in Perspective*
Robert R. Sterling and Arthur L. Thomas (Editors), *Accounting for a Simplified Firm Owning Depreciable Assets*
Reed K. Storey, *The Search for Accounting Principles*
Study Group on Business Income, *Changing Concepts of Business Income*

THE INTERPRETATION OF ACCOUNTS

(STAMP-MARTIN PAPERS)

F. SEWELL BRAY

STAMP-MARTIN PROFESSOR OF ACCOUNTING

Scholars Book Co.
4431 Mt. Vernon
Houston, Texas 77006

Reprinted 1979 by Scholars Book Co.

Library of Congress Cataloging in Publication Data

Bray, Frank Sewell.
The interpretation of accounts (Stamp-Martin papers)

(Accounting classics series)
Reprint of the ed. published for the Incorporated Accountants' Research Committee by Oxford University Press, London, New York.
1. Accounting. I. Title.
[HF5635.B8344 1979] 657 79-22380
ISBN 0-914348-29-9

Printed in the United States of America

To the memory of

MRS. M. E. ROBINSON

Sometime Fellow of
Newnham College, Cambridge
and sometime lecturer in economics at
Birkbeck College, London

FOREWORD

The accountancy profession is increasingly liberating itself from the status of being merely the provider of skilled recording services and is becoming concerned with the interpretation and use of accounts.

The direction and speed of progress may depend on the reconciliation of three divergent views about the purposes of accounts.

Firstly, accounts may be regarded as being primarily related to business needs, for the guidance of the managements of individual enterprises. *Secondly*, because accountants are much influenced by contemporary legal requirements, accounting forms may be primarily related to the Companies Act and to tax legislation. *Thirdly*, fundamental methods of classification and valuation in accounting forms may be influenced by the views of economists, who have discovered the merits of accounting technique as a method of analysis.

The divergent nature of these views can be clearly seen in relation to such current problems as the calculation of true profits, stock valuation methods and the treatment of changing money values. Entirely different results are produced according to which of the three views is predominant. The whole purpose of Professor Bray's book is to suggest that the three viewpoints can be reconciled and that, if the accountancy profession is willing to think about fundamental theory, sets of accounts can be designed which will satisfy all requirements.

Much of Professor Bray's work is related to Social Accounting—the method by which our familiar technique of double-entry is used to aggregate the financial transactions of all the individuals, all the departments of government, and all the corporate bodies which, together, make up the society or the nation. Since some of his concepts may be unfamiliar to those accustomed to traditional accounting technique, it may be convenient to summarize here the main differences between Social Accounting and Business Accounting, as dealt with in Raymond Goldsmith's Princeton *Study of Saving in the United States*:

(*a*) A relevant fact, to be recorded by the system of accounts, is determined in social accounting by considerations of economic theory and not by the habits guiding business accountants, who in this respect are influenced primarily by contemporary legal arrangements.

(*b*) Social accounting places much greater emphasis on standardization and consistency than business accounting does.

(*c*) Social accounting is not bound in the same way to the acceptance of the legal monetary unit of time and place as business accounting.

(*d*) Social accounting is free to deviate in other respects too from the customary procedures of business accounting if considerations of economic theory call for it.

(*e*) For social accounting the economy as a whole is a permanent entity with an infinitely long life. In business accounting many procedures are still influenced by its origin in the recording of short-term ventures.

(*f*) Social accounting is not guided by the 'principle of conservatism' which is of such importance in business accounting, a principle exemplified by the customary valuation of inventory at cost or market, whichever is lower.

As the reviewer of Mr. Goldsmith's book in *The Accounting Review* said: 'All accountants might well speculate on whether financial accounting would not be improved if these differences were lessened. Traditional accounting has much to learn from social accounting and much to contribute to it.'

My hope is that this desirable development will be helped by this book by Professor Bray, who is doing such notable pioneer work in this field.

BERTRAM NELSON

President of The Society of Incorporated Accountants

CONTENTS

FOREWORD BY THE PRESIDENT OF THE SOCIETY vii

ACKNOWLEDGEMENTS x

PART ONE

1. AN ACCOUNTING PROGRESSION 3
2. THE FORMAL PRINCIPLES OF PUBLIC COMPANY ACCOUNTING 19
3. ACCOUNTING DYNAMICS—I 41
4. ACCOUNTING DYNAMICS—II 70
5. ACCOUNTING DYNAMICS—III 86
6. ACCOUNTING DYNAMICS—IV 105
7. BASIC CONCEPTS IN ACCOUNTING—Economic Accounting: A study in Conceptional Relationships 129
8. CAPITAL CHANGES 161

PART TWO

9. THE NATURE AND PURPOSE OF DIRECT TAXATION 179
10. AUDITING THEORY 190
11. A FORMAL REVIEW OF SOCIAL ACCOUNTING 199

ACKNOWLEDGEMENTS

I thank the editors of *Accounting Research*, *The Manager*, *The Incorporated Statistician*, *The Accountant*, *Accountancy*, and *The Accountants' Magazine*, for permission to reproduce papers which they published.

F. S. B.

PART ONE

I

AN ACCOUNTING PROGRESSION

The inaugural lecture of the First Stamp-Martin Professor of Accounting delivered at Incorporated Accountants Hall, London, on 17th March, 1953

1. An inaugural lecture should have some of the qualities of a Caroline sermon. You may remember that Isaac Barrow[1] was eminent as a mathematician as well as being one of the greatest of the Caroline divines. He was Professor of Greek at Cambridge in 1660, becoming in 1663 the first Professor of Mathematics, resigning in 1669 in favour of his pupil, Isaac Newton.[2] I feel, therefore, that I am in the best of company in proposing to you three texts.

First—'The Roman soldier who killed Archimedes was a symbol of the death of original thought that Rome caused throughout the Hellenic world.'—Bertrand Russell.[3]

Second—'. . . to find causal judgments that are universally true is notoriously a matter of extreme difficulty. The late date at which most of the physical sciences became exact, and the comparative fewness of the laws which they have succeeded in establishing even now, are sufficient proofs of this difficulty.' —Professor G. E. Moore.[4]

Third—'. . . in the most extreme case . . . 'knowledge' can be the manipulation of a pattern of symbols for correlating experiences.'—Martin Johnson.[5]

2. It is only fitting that on this particular occasion I should pay homage to a great act of imagination on the part of the Council of

[1] 1630–77.

[2] See note in *Selected English Sermons* (Oxford University Press—The World's Classics), p. 166.

[3] *History of Western Philosophy* (Allen & Unwin, London, 1946), p. 240.

[4] *Principia Ethica* (Cambridge University Press, fourth impression, 1948), p. 22.

[5] *Time and Universe for the Scientific Conscience*—Sixth Eddington Memorial Lecture (Cambridge University Press, 1952), p. 22.

the Society of Incorporated Accountants in founding this Chair. It is marked by honoured and venerated names, and secured in its status by the counsel of academic advisers, whose several claims to distinction are known. Anyone faced with the first occupancy of a foundation carrying with it a depth of aim and ambition must feel a sense of deep responsibility. Indeed, without it there can be little hope for the realization of those ideals which brought it into being.

3. Professorial responsibility calls for intellectual belief in a subject, and I affirm my belief in accounting. I think it will always hold its own with other disciplines. Belief implies faith and the future of any profession—especially if it should claim to be a learned one—must depend upon the development of either the art or science which it practises, but without faith there can never be development. We have no need to be ashamed of accounting. It is indispensable to civilized society. Has there ever been economic activity in the real world which has not required the preparation of some form of account? As long as men exchange goods and services they will always want accounts to give them succinct views of their transactions.

4. The Stamp-Martin Chair has great significance. It will further the cause of accounting research in a spirit of freedom. Freedom and independence are essential conditions for the promotion of good research work because they let in the ideas of other domains of reasoning. If my own mental preferences favour economics and philosophy, that is not to say I disdain the ideas of other disciplines. Although I do not set on one side their usefulness and necessity, yet I have no lasting hope in the powers of purely narrow technical inquiries to secure the intellectual permanence of accounting as an academic subject. Surely an applied art like accounting *can* be thought of as the outer garment of a moral science, but much meditation will be required before it can be made to yield its possibilities in that shape.

5. In part, I shall try to pursue my own thinking in the way of that approach, and I shall hope some of it may show in the research lectures which I am to deliver in this Hall, but I also want to make it clear that I shall not overlook the link between practice and

research. Moreover, I want to help forward any proposals which are designed to bring about a closer union between the profession and those universities which are prepared to find a home for accounting. Professional and academic accountants have much to offer each other, and the development of a closer understanding between them must result in capital gains. I want to hold a number of seminars at which experienced accountants drawn from practice, industry, government, and the teaching world can exchange ideas, and give to research students the benefits of their hopes for the future. I think of discussions on such questions as the simplification of public company accounts; interpretation, expectation and prediction as thought of in relation to all kinds of accounting; and the auditing standards applicable to public companies. I sometimes think that adequate disclosure to protect investors is more a matter of auditing standards than of statutory compulsion, and I cannot but feel that such information as comes to light after an accounting date must bear upon any report, still to be made, which purports to affirm a true and fair view at that date.

6. It has always seemed to me that accounting would benefit if those who teach the subject, and guide its research, would give some time to the preparation of a few carefully written texts. We need books which express clearly and simply the underlying ideas and basic concepts of accounting procedures. It is still difficult to come upon a really adequate introduction to the subject, and even at this time of day we hear quite educated people disclaiming all knowledge of accounts. I hope my academic colleagues are at one with me in a desire to improve upon this situation. A good subject deserves a good bibliography.

7. I believe we are in need of more results acquired from factual studies. Reliable research students should have opportunities for collecting information in the real world. I instance one type of problem which has not been adequately met by factual study. What is the effect of high income taxation on long term productivity? For example, I am suspicious of a type of comparison which always implies that some of us must work harder. Output depends upon capital inputs as well as labour inputs, and in the long run the continued presence of effective operating assets is a

matter of saving and investment, in the economic connotations of those terms. Intuitively we sense that some measures of taxation have been pressed too far, perhaps beyond the limits of stability. It may well be that we are provoking relatively decreasing output standards as a by-product of fiscal policy. As time goes on I shall try to ask a number of questions which might be answered in the light of collections of facts taken from accounts, and it is my hope that like minded students may wish to investigate them with me. In a pleasantly revealing passage, Lord Stamp once said:

> If out of every five young accountants who 'take an interest in economic and social questions' only one will deny himself the more exciting pleasures of debating societies, parliaments, or the grateful temperatures of public platform exposition, where generalities are dealt in and acuteness of intellect promoted, and that one will pursue the more prosaic path of establishing exact knowledge by passing in review the data that come before him in his profession, and presenting us with a coefficient of dispersion or a coefficient of correlation which will have a definite meaning to us, then in a decade economic science will have an exactness and precision that it lacks today.[1]

If the time interval in this assertion seems agreeably optimistic at least the idea was cogent. So much then for some of my plans for the future.

8. This lecture gives me a chance to review foundations before I reflect upon possibilities. I think accounting is one of the most important of applied economic techniques because it gives a representation of the working of the economic system at whatever point you care to look at it. As brought to maturity in the enterprises of the real world it has dealt with known transactions, and those economic happenings which can be measured by imputation from known transactions. It is now grappling with expected transactions and sooner or later it will have to face some measurement problems associated with ideas and concepts relevant to those misplaced and unrecorded costs and benefits which never enter into exchange transactions. I therefore regard accounting as one of those arts which make for stability and order in the life of

[1] *Studies in Current Problems in Finance and Government* (P. S. King & Son Ltd., London, 1924), p. 25.

economic society. Occasionally we meet criticism of a philosophical kind. It is said that accounting comparisons are useless when you are investigating unlike entities; unlike because they are operating under different sanctions having different values at their source. If it is the comparison which is in point we should probably agree, although there can be reservations when like activities are contrasted, but when we are told that ascetic societies constituted by notions of poverty can do without accounts, then it is time to call a halt. If an ascetic community consistently overspends even a slender income it will eventually disintegrate as an entity in itself.

9. As a consequence of this type of criticism, I take the view that we should have another look at the work which accounts are designed to do; in other words, what are their primary functions? I know I have dealt with these before, but because of their importance and the salient fact that we should never lose sight of them, they will bear repetition. I make out six functions based on a few fundamental concepts:

i. To give a clear record of and to measure income from economic activity.
ii. To show how far operating activity has been effectively carried out.
iii. To reveal the effect and measurements of income transfers.
iv. To control outlay by measurements of spending and saving.
v. To show the uses to which saving has been put and to measure capital changes.
vi. To give an inventory of assets and liabilities and to measure the wealth and credit standing of an entity of account.

10. Accounting, as we have known it, has been closely allied to the law, from which it derives and observes an opinion on stewardship, as well as a variety of fiscal views on the direct taxation of incomes. Quite early on in the span of its life which most of us here can remember, it was confronted with pricing problems involving the delineation of product costs. These were

largely the derivatives of its being. They still are, but we begin to see the boundaries extending. Measurement ideas are starting to worry accountants, yet it is only in comparatively recent years that we have heard talk of principles. I think we must all agree that accounting is only just now becoming aware of itself. The signs are unmistakable. Those management problems which are pressing hard upon the heels of accountants everywhere do not call for new subjects with strange qualifying titles to accounting proper. What is needed is a fundamental understanding of the one subject, so that interpretation, expectation, prediction, and the building up of significant aggregates may be securely grounded on those concepts and functions which our thinking and experience force us to look upon as valid approximations to truth. Therefore, we should never let our students be over-examined in a variety of so-called techniques at the expense of a proper education in the *one* subject.

11. And now I want to consider, if I may, the accounting implications of expectation and prediction. In this context I think there will be some of you who will look upon prediction as far too sharp and precise a word for denoting the kind of thing that goes on in counting-houses. Very well then, for those who prefer it I substitute the word forecasting. In my Balliol address on Accounting Form[1] I tried to establish a form of operating account which might be regarded as explicitly fundamental, and if you will bear with me I should like to give you a short description of its make-up. The design is simple. The account has four columns bearing the titles—actual, the expectation, tolerance limits, variance beyond tolerance. Perhaps I should explain that tolerance limits are thought of in terms of standard deviations calculated from past figures. The account is divided into two parts, one of which deals with variable inputs and output. Output is defined in value-added terms to mean the sales or market values of goods and services produced, minus direct purchase acquisitions of goods and services, plus or minus an adjustment for changes in inventories. In passing, I think we should observe how strangely this measure of output fits in with that venerable notion of a merchant's gross

[1] *Four Essays in Accounting Theory* (Oxford University Press, 1953).

profit which so many of us were brought up on. I know that this concept of output or value added involves some valuation problems, but I want to reserve these for another occasion. Variable inputs are defined in the factor category of labour as wages, salaries and social insurance contributions and are classified as: (1) direct or operative; (2) ancillary; and (3) selling and distribution.

12. In general terms we can say that these inputs move more or less proportionately with output, so that if we *can* make a fair estimate of the latter, past experience should provide us with reliable estimates of the former on the grounds of regular occurrence. I think it is important to check these estimates with the aid of statistical techniques. Nevertheless, despite the suggestion of proportional movement it has to be remembered that in this part of the operating account the variable margin between inputs and output is only maximized when marginal cost is equal to marginal revenue. When we are dealing with efficiently managed entities, estimates of variable inputs are less problematical, apart from relative price changes, than anything we may conjecture for output. Yet, for all that, the output or value added of a firm can be related to a functional analysis of sales and purchases in the Leontief manner, by indicating those areas of activity from whence it buys and those to whom it sells. Forecasting in some measure depends upon knowledge of the association of the behaviour of those realms of activity with general economic conditions and with changes in the structure of the social accounts, in particular the constitution of the national income and its disposal. As Mr. Friday has very plainly pointed out:

The reliability of the forecast will depend on having available the maximum amount of knowledge and of being blessed with that flair called good judgment, which comes from long experience as much as from some special quality of the mind. The economist in industry can help in providing much of the required knowledge, but not all of it. Only the sales staff are likely to possess an intimate knowledge of customers' preferences and requirements, necessary for forecasting the demand for the firm's own products. On the other hand, the economist will possess a knowledge and experience of interpreting economic events which others in the firm will not have. The economist can, therefore, collect all the required knowledge about general economic conditions in all the territories in which the firm trades and information about the market for the product concerned. The more knowledge we possess the better should be our forecast. The economist may well make good forecasts of cost changes and of the demand for the product in the whole market. The sales manager is certainly best fitted to forecast his share of that total demand. The dilemma which faces business men is that they must make forecasts in detail, in order to plan factory output, yet they cannot eliminate forecasting errors. It is this uncertainty about the future which makes business risky and puts a premium on the person with sound judgment.[1]

He therefore concludes that 'Good forecasting is an art', and I do not think that any of us can gainsay him.

13. The second part of my operating account centres attention upon the claims on the variable margin. These claims may be classified as purchases of goods and services related to operating facilities, but not directly varying with output; wages, salaries, other remuneration and social insurance contributions allocated to administration and management; and capital inputs in the shape of imputed or actual rents of factory, warehouse, sales-room and office, as well as depreciation of *real* assets. The balancing item in this part of the account is described as operating income. It will be seen that for the most part the claims on the variable margin are composed of standing charges with some admixture of semi-variable expense. Once we have decided that the standing charges are at an effective minimum for the scale of output contemplated then we should not meet insuperable difficulties in the way of reliable estimation. We know from experience that semi-variable expense can be another matter, especially when we are dealing with hundreds of items for something like the maintenance of heavy equipment. In a large organization it is quite possible to be badly out in an estimate of maintenance expenditure, made up of goods and services, just because the size and number of suppliers' accounts is not properly comprehended at the start. To get over this kind of mistake it is wise to work on carefully selected samples

[1] 'The Problem of Business Forecasting', by Frank A. Friday. *The Journal of Industrial Economics*, Vol. 1, November, 1952. No. 1, p. 71.

of entries in order to check the influence of a wide range of small accounts, and to see that that influence is not under- or over-estimated. I owe this suggestion to Mr. A. W. Swan. But when all is said and done it is *not* this part of the operating account which presents the real uncertainties to mar figures of expectation and prediction. These lie in the first part of the account and hinge upon the forecasts of output. Although we cannot replace qualities of sound judgement by investigations into consumer demand and by the use of statistical methods, yet I do think we need to think about and to classify as many causal relationships as research can uncover. Much would be gained if experienced firms would make available to *bona fide* research investigators the background study undertaken, the prediction methods employed, and the degrees of reliability of their own attempts at output forecasts.

14. I have sought to deflect attention to expectations of output because it has seemed to me that cost accounting in the past decade or so has been over preoccupied with cost control. At bottom all the major ideas associated with so-called standard costing are centred upon cost control, and although I do not minimize its importance in the interests of productive efficiency, I still feel that it is only one side of all that I should wish to find in expectation accounting. I advance the view that costing first came into vogue as an aid to product pricing. It soon came to be recognized that industrial effectiveness depended upon an intimate knowledge of divisional operating costs, and as this phase developed accountants hit upon the idea that control was best exercised by the predetermination of what such costs ought to be in relation to what in fact they turned out to be. The difference or variance between the two became a measure of ineffectiveness demanding a probing inquiry followed by redressing action. This transition in costing ideas is clearly brought out in the best book I have read on the subject. I refer to the report of the Cost Accounting Subcommittee of the Taxation and Financial Relations Committee of the Institute.[1] Thus:

[1] *Developments in Cost Accounting*. Report of the Cost Accounting Subcommittee of the Taxation and Financial Relations Committee of the Institute of Chartered Accountants in England and Wales (Gee & Co. (Publishers) Ltd., 1947).

It is, in fact, one of the most important conclusions we have reached that sound costing technique places the same emphasis on cost control as on cost ascertainment.[1]

And again:

The most essential purpose of cost accounting is that of providing accurate and prompt information and cost data in order that management may be placed in a position to control cost per unit of output for all elements of cost, both direct and overhead expense. Such control implies the promotion of efficiency, e.g. in the usage of labour, materials and machines, by providing management with appropriate information as to production per man—or machine-hour, idle man—or machine-hours, material consumption, wastage, rejects, and special losses or gains peculiar to the industry, such as those due to humidity. Competition establishes selling prices to a large degree, and the profit-earning capacity of a particular organization may be influenced materially by the efficiency with which costs are controlled.[2]

I think that both cost ascertainment and cost control influence selling prices and I do agree that another main purpose of cost accounting

is to provide: (i) a basis for estimating; (ii) information enabling the accuracy of all estimates to be checked; in other words, the dual function of cost estimation and ascertainment.[3]

Nevertheless,I feel that the protagonists of cost control tend to pin their whole faith on a thorough understanding of the input side of the operating account. This alone will not suffice. What *is* wanted is a thorough understanding of all those implications which attach to *both* sides of the account. The output side upon which all costs depend is the vital 'moment' in the situation. It has the primacy because *there* is the point of uncertainty. The solutions to the problems of expectation accounting lie in the synthesis I have indicated, but the order is first output and *then* inputs.

15. I think we can now say that cost control is becoming well understood, and its methods are approaching some maturity. I like the ideas associated with work study and the general concept of programming which they conjure up. In the way of ordering

[1] *Developments in Cost Accounting*, p. 9. [2] *Ibid.*, p. 17. [3] *Ibid.*, p. 18.

these ideas there is much to be said for the kind of report which has been recently put out by the joint committee of the Institute of Cost and Works Accountants and the Institution of Production Engineers.[1] Anything which does something to promote effective minimum marginal costs and minimum effective standing charges must be supported. I think we should all agree that matters of expectation and policy demand a concentration upon essentials, and time to think out their relevance. Accounts prepared for those so engaged should only deal with essentials, but there are other levels of management who want to be kept up to the mark. I therefore welcome the statement in the report I have cited that:

> By publishing information emphasizing those factors that require action and by recommending the nature of the action, the work study department can often take over the watching of day-to-day trends, thus leaving management more free to develop long term policy and plan future projects. At the same time, supervisors at all levels can be supplied with the information necessary for them to exercise a degree of control that would otherwise be impossible.[2]

16. The advantages of cost control are plainly apparent in large-scale organizations and—dare I say it—nationalized undertakings, but they still need simple development in their application to both small- and medium-sized enterprises. For myself, I think that cost variances can be elementally classified into those which *are* controllable, those which depend upon volume, and those which show unsuspected fixed expense deviation. Controllable variances are plainly matters for direct investigation and are very much in line with work study notions. They are pointers to straight *operating* effectiveness and all supervisory managers should take note of them. Volume variances come right up against my references to output, and emphasize the effects of mistaken estimates of demand. Executives concerned with policy decisions must watch them closely. Fixed expense variances press upon the consequence of keeping standing charges to that minimum level which is compatible with effectiveness. Administrators must fasten on to and correct them.

[1] *Measurement of Productivity—Work Study Application and Training.*
[2] *Ibid.*, p. 17.

17. I have always been an exponent of uniformity in the presentation of operating accounts and cost statements. Different presentations founded upon different bases of allocation, for like firms in the same industry, do not aid necessary factual comparisons. It is one of the faults of medium- to small-scale enterprise that independence in the classification and formal presentation of operating aggregates is sometimes counted a virtue. Accounts which are complicated and awkward to understand are usually the result of indifferent accounting knowledge. As I commented at the Society's Balliol course in September of last year: 'The more clear-headed and fundamental our understanding of these things the fewer will be our categories and therefore the simpler and more straightforward will be our forms of account.' This is a matter of some importance for small firms in an industry. If their operating accounts and cost statements are simple and logical it facilitates meaningful aggregations by central organizations like trade associations. As it is they can impair these aggregations at a time when they are becoming more and more useful as factual evidence in answering a variety of questions put to those responsible for the leadership of the industry as a whole. For example, what is the contribution of the particular industry to the economy as a whole? What are the input-output relations with other industries, or differently constituted organizations in the same industry? Moreover firms will benefit if aggregate indicators in percentage terms are supported by measures of standard deviation to mark the limits of normal activity, and when it comes to a consideration of specific cost aggregates the more advanced firms may want a pointer to the lowest, and perhaps the highest, operators contributing to the aggregation. Again, it is not altogether irrelevant to suggest that both product and process costings should be façades of the same system; the one should never be over-emphasized at the expense of the other.

There is still much room for the development of order in the accounting presentations of firms within industries, and there is *indeed* room for a better understanding of significant relationships between aggregate categories in accounts.

18. I turn to other matters and I have a suspicion that my

present auditors will not willingly dismiss me from an *inaugural* lecture if I fail to make at least some reference to the burning questions of the day. I refer to the accounting implications of changing money values. I have lived with these problems for so long now that I tend to think of them as theoretically settled. I know that in the world of practical affairs the battle still rages, and I count it as something of a triumph for academic discussion that these issues should have been brought thus far. If you are prepared to regard accounting as concerned with means of measurement to be brought into touch with an intelligible system of accounts then, as it seems to me, you must encompass the effects of changing price levels in order that accounting forms may claim some of the qualities to be discerned in formal relationships.

I am one of the people who do believe in ideas commonly associated with objective measures of income and capital. I think I have said before that no one is really going to make me believe that conceptually business income is somehow different from personal income, or that the *capital* employed by the owners of a business is different from the *capital* employed *in* a business because of the incidence of borrowed money or long-term claims. If you are really concerned with an asset-income relationship then you should seek measures for operating assets and finance employed rather than impose an ambiguity on the term 'capital employed'. I still think we must get down to fundamental concepts unconfused by side issues. When we have made up our minds on that score we should strive to think out the accounting means of measurement which come as close to those concepts as we can get them. No doubt we shall only work out approximations, but as time goes on we hope to improve them. The important point to remember is that we shall never achieve anything of scientific consequence unless we *do* set these conceptual goals.

19. I am told that the problem of stock valuation is bothering some accountants more than the twin issue posed by the depreciation of fixed assets. I propose, therefore, to set on one side the depreciation question and confine myself to a simple way of looking at the stock problem. It is my view that we should understand accounts far better if we concentrated our attention upon changes

in real aggregates rather than on aggregate classifications themselves. I think we must all agree that the measurement of the profit of an accounting period is materially affected by changes in the opening and closing inventories of stock and work in progress. It therefore seems to me that that part of the total stock and work in progress associated with operating activity, which is consumed in an accounting period, negative formation as the economists call it, should be evaluated by reference to present values at the terminal date. Contrariwise an increase in the total stock and work in progress associated with operating activity in an accounting period, that is, positive formation, should be evaluated either at cost on a last-in basis or by reference to lower present values at the terminal date. In this way of doing things the objective measurement of profit is related to changes in total inventories valued on a last cost basis and not to the variable first costs or lower market values of opening and closing inventories. I feel reasonably confident on the theory of the matter whatever we choose to do about it in practice.

20. A short time ago I tried to re-state the fundamental principles of accounting, and in doing so I left out two working rules which are usually taken for principles. I refer to the application of accounting periods from which we derive our notions of accrual and deferment, and the dependence of income measurement on realization involving a cost sterilization of uncompleted transactions. I must make it clear that I see nothing particularly amiss with either of these rules. It is plainly our first duty to bring order and meaning into all recorded transactions which have taken place under one roof over a given period of time. The resulting epitomizations are essential factual presentations which tell their story within the limits of a static interval of time. They cannot be denied on any showing of stewardship, and they bring to notice some indispensable restrictions on business behaviour, but they do *not* complacently reveal *causal* or necessarily dependent relationships between categories. It may be that eventually those engaged in expectation accounting will want to know something about these relationships if, in fact, they can be shown to exist. For example, it might well be that real asset formation is for some entities

induced by the trend of past outputs, accumulated saving and the present borrowing potential, rather than by current output and current saving. Yet again, for some members of society current consumption may depend upon penultimate rather than current incomes. I therefore advance the suggestion that such mental models as use aggregate variables drawn from customary accounts, and which rely upon functional lags to secure their premises, might be cast in special accounting forms made independent of the usual formal time period. Much thinking allied to factual research will be needed before we can ever make use of any such symbolic representation of accounts, but I do not put it outside the range of probability.

Among other things, stewardship is concerned with conservation, and it is only natural and proper that accounts designed for the owners of an enterprise should look upon realized increment as the primary requisite of income distribution, but when it comes to a use of accounts which looks to their make-up for criteria of effectiveness, then sterilized cost aggregates may have to give place to valued aggregates, even though valuation is not a delicate instrument of certainty.

21. You will gather from what I have said that there will be some research studies proceeding on the following lines:

i. An investigation into economic presentations of enterprise accounts.
ii. An inquiry into the relationships between fundamental categories in accounts (*a*) as criteria of effectiveness and (*b*) as a means of comprehending possible causal patterns.

I expect that some of this work will be done at Cambridge, where I am continuing my association with the Department of Applied Economics. I also think it will be worth while to look into a new conception of form. I refer to accounting for *changes* in categories. I believe there is a strong case to be made out for a study of accounting changes, both on capital and current accounts, and I see in it some relevance to the kind of work which is going on in the economic field on such subjects as the theory of investment of the firm, and preferred asset ratios.

22. It is often said that education is best served by a study of the humanities, and not by the promotion of new subjects, especially those with a technical bent. I must say that only the other day, I was surprised to hear it re-affirmed by a scholar who graduated in Canada, and thereafter proceeded by way of Harvard to Cambridge, and then to London. His subject shall be nameless, but he repeated the familiar story of the Cambridge mathematician who took pride in reminding those who were listening to him in a senior combination room that he had never achieved anything useful. This disregard for the utilitarian awakes an echo of sympathy in all of us who would want to find truth, but it overlooks the probability that we may come upon much the same kind of *universal* propositions to give *any* subject order and meaning, if we only pursue a subject deeply enough. In a recent after-dinner speech the Master of the Rolls made mention of the place of scholarship and learning in the accountancy profession. It is the purpose of this foundation to secure that place.

2

THE FORMAL PRINCIPLES OF PUBLIC COMPANY ACCOUNTING

A research lecture given at Incorporated Accountants Hall, London, on 19th October, 1953

1. As you will judge from the title which I have chosen for this research lecture, I propose to re-examine the general characteristics of public company accounts, and especially the make-up of these documents, as matters of form. It has been said of one of my patrons that he had great practice 'in analysing financial results and clarifying the administrative problems raised',[1] and if we look for the source of these abilities, we find that Stamp had clear ideas about the formal principles of any subject, accounting or otherwise, that he happened to be considering. He literally knew the form, and if I may be permitted one early digression, I should like to comment, yet again, on the importance of Form. You may remember that at Oxford last year, I drew attention to Schrödinger's view of Form as a fundamental concept, and I sought to develop this in relation to those mental models which are constituted by accounts. Perhaps I should add that, so far as concerns the form of accounts shortly to be considered, an attempt will be made to build from fundamental concepts, so far as this is possible, rather than to rely upon a structure shaped solely to comply with those legal sanctions which result from a few practical lessons. It was Aquinas who likened pure meanings to forms and who said that 'anything can be examined free from non-essential involvements, and therefore the forms and meanings of things, though committed to a changing reality, can be considered as invariable in themselves, and ascertainable by scientific definition. . . .'[2]

2. There are two simple propositions which essentially inform all planned arrangements of aggregate transactions. Although

[1] Sir Henry Clay on Lord Stamp.

[2] *Philosophical Texts*, selected and translated by Thomas Gilby (Oxford University Press, 1951), No. 44, p. 17.

derived from national accounting, they are relevant to public company accounting because they contain the minimum elements of a pure theory of accounting. We can never get away from them, and therefore they must be re-stated. Thus, in general terms, and in a given time period, income is devoted to consumption expenditure and saving, and saving is resolved in capital formation. Public companies are not usually final consumers, so that we can rule out consumption expenditure, and that leaves us with income, saving and capital as the minimum elements in public company accounting. These minimum elements are generally expressed in a set of formally related accounts: one, to measure period income, two, to reveal transfers of income and the measurement of saving, three, to explain the application of saving, and four, to measure capital as a stock.[1]

3. Let us now consider the nature of those transactions which are the subject matter of public company accounting. I think we must all recognize that real resources and their utilization are the mainspring of economic activity, but it is equally important to remember that real resources cannot be acquired and put into use without finance. We know that the first duty of accounting is the plain recording of the incomings and outgoings of entities, both real and financial, and that these originating transactions are the subject of a preliminary sorting 'as between those which carry significance in relation to a time period intentionally set for . . . short review, and those which are . . . less immediate in the sense of either internal durability conceived by the quality of delayed and gradual movement into the flow of the current, or exclusion by reason of external qualities of independence,' i.e. fixed asset and financial claim transactions. This preliminary sorting of transactions broadly corresponds to a primary descriptive accounting differentiation between those items which relate to current account and those which relate to capital account, those which are destined to find their place in the income or profit and loss account, and those which find their place in the balance sheet.[2] You will also

[1] Cf. *Four Essays in Accounting Theory* (Oxford University Press, 1953), p. 6.

[2] Cf. *The Measurement of Profit* (Oxford University Press, 1949; second impression, 1953), p. 10.

remember that in my previous lecture I said of accounting that 'as brought to maturity in the enterprises of the real world it has dealt with known transactions, and those economic happenings which can be measured by imputation from known transactions'. I went on to say that 'it is now grappling with expected transactions and sooner or later it will have to face some measurement problems associated with ideas and concepts relevant to those misplaced and unrecorded costs and benefits which never enter into exchange transactions. I therefore regard accounting as one of those arts which make for stability and order in the life of economic society.' Expected transactions are the intimate concern of management accounting, and they will be left out of this discussion because *our* immediate concern is with the financial accounts of public companies.

4. This short survey suggests that, apart from the distinction between current and capital, the transactions of public companies can be classified in the following manner:

i. Real transactions with a monetary consummation.
ii. Financial or credit transactions.
iii. Imputed transactions.
iv. Non-monetary transactions (i.e. real transactions without a monetary consummation).

Real with a monetary consummation mainly refers to purchases and sales of goods and services, recorded at the times of transfers of title, at the monetary values then placed upon them, i.e. the amounts of money due and assignable in respect of goods delivered and services rendered to or by a company during a given period of account. Financial or credit relates to transactions in debt and financial assets. Imputed refers to those transactions which do not arise from exchanges between entities. Thus, depreciation resulting from the use of fixed assets is an imputed transaction, as is also a rent charge for owner-occupied buildings. Non-monetary relates to transactions in kind, e.g. directors' benefits received otherwise than in cash.

5. Modern accounts are epitomizations of real, financial,

imputed and non-monetary transactions. The great majority of transactions can all be brought under the basic descriptions of real and financial. This has important consequences inasmuch as the distinction between real transactions and financial transactions is quite fundamental, and *that* for the reasons I have several times mentioned in *Four Essays in Accounting Theory*.[1] Professor Ragnar Frisch has impressed upon us 'the necessity of making a thorough distinction between flows in real objects and financial objects'. In fact he seems to have 'decided never to accept any system of concepts where this distinction is not made in a clear-cut fashion'.[2] It is true that in making these remarks he was specifically referring to work on national accounting, its principles and logical foundation, nevertheless it seems to me that they are sufficiently universal to be relevant to any kind of accounting. Again, it is equally clear that reasonable measures of income and capital, and of some of the aggregate categories in their make-up, are only possible when due account is taken of estimates for both imputed and non-monetary transactions. The former are usually none the less real, and plainly the latter are always real. The English Companies Act of 1948 has something to say on both classes of transactions, but in case it should be thought that non-monetary transactions are unimportant we should bear in mind the specific reference to the *estimated money value* of any other benefits received by a director otherwise than in cash, in the disclosure requirements relating to directors' emoluments, Section 196 (2).

Before leaving this discussion on the nature of transactions, I think it is still instructive to look once again at a simple but fundamental view of real transactions with a monetary consummation, and for this purpose I would like to make use of the explanation given by Professor Ruggles, of Yale. He says that:

> Every transaction necessarily involves both a buyer and a seller, and each of these must take account of two different aspects of the transaction.

[1] Oxford University Press, 1953, e.g. pp. 9–10.

[2] Discussion on the relationship between input-output analysis and national accounting by Richard Stone and J. E. G. Utting in *Input-Output Relations: Proceedings of a Conference on Inter-Industrial Relations held at Driebergen, Holland*, p. 228 (Netherlands Economic Institute, 1953)—Department of Applied Economics, University of Cambridge, Reprint Series, No. 70.

The buyer must record (1) that money (or some equivalent) has been given up and (2) that additional goods have been received. The seller, on the other hand, must record (1) that goods have left the firm and (2) that payment for them has been received. These entries on the part of the buyer and the seller represent the four different aspects of the transaction.... In summary, then, every transaction will have four complete aspects. In the first place, it will appear in the accounts of two different firms or individuals. In the second place, in the accounts of each of these firms or individuals, it will appear twice, once to show the goods or services exchanged and once to show the payment for it. All four of these aspects will be equal, and all four must be shown if the transaction is to be recorded completely.[1]

The nature of transactions themselves, when taken in conjunction with the simple propositions enumerated in paragraph 2, suggest that the important aggregate measures required from public company accounting are those of real income, financial income, total income, retained income, capital formation, changes in financial claims, aggregate real worth, net aggregate financial claims and total capital.

6. The next step is to consider the major uses of public company accounts. It is worth recalling that Mr. G. O. May has suggested at least ten distinguishable uses which can be recognized for financial accounts, but I do not think all of them can be *directly* associated with the published accounts of public companies in this country. I shall first re-state Mr. May's list, and then I shall abstract from, and add to it, for the purposes of this discussion. The ten uses given by Mr. May are:

i. As a report of stewardship.
ii. As a basis for fiscal policy.
iii. To determine the legality of dividends.
iv. As a guide to wise dividend action.
v. As a basis for the granting of credit.
vi. As information for prospective investors in an enterprise.
vii. As a guide to the value of investments already made.

[1] *An Introduction to National Income and Income Analysis*, by Richard Ruggles (McGraw-Hill Book Company, Inc., 1949), pp. 23–4.

viii. As an aid to Government supervision.
ix. As a basis for price or rate regulation.
x. As a basis for taxation.[1]

He later remarks that: 'Financial statements are usually intended to bc acted upon, and once issued they may be put to any one of the many uses by those into whose hands they come. They are significant even more on account of the inferences that are likely to be drawn from them on account of their character as statements of fact or opinion.'[2] I think we readily accept these comments, and recognize the accounting responsibilities which they imply.

Financial writers are never tired of telling us that public company accounts are published for shareholders.[3] As a consequence, therefore, items one, three, four, six and seven must take precedence in Mr. May's list. We should notice that three and four are materially concerned with income distribution, and this at once suggests the importance of a total income measure. Sometimes it seems that too little attention is paid to the significance of a total capital measure, and certainly far more consideration might be given to capital changes than would seem to be the case at present. I shall have more to say on these questions later, but perhaps I may add the comment here that I do not very readily subscribe to the view that balance sheets are little more than the links between successive income statements.

Published company accounts *do* influence the granting of credit,

[1] *Financial Accounting*, by George O. May (New York, The Macmillan Company, 1943), p. 3.

[2] *Ibid.*, p. 19.

[3] As a partial commentary on this, it is interesting to notice Keirstead's view of a corporation as seen through the eyes of a chief executive. He says that: 'It is an organisation, much greater than himself, into which he projects himself, but it is a distinct entity, not by any means an association of equity shareholders. It has its own life, its own greatness, in which the entrepreneur participates, and, most important, it has its own interest to be served. The entrepreneur may say, and believe, when he speaks at the company meeting, and is reported in *The Times*, that the interests of the company are the interests of the shareholders, but his ordinary thoughts do not run along these lines. Most of the time the company which he serves has its own interest to which he dedicates himself. (The shareholders will benefit if the company is successful, but their benefit is, so to speak, incidental.)' *An Essay in the Theory of Profits and Income Distribution*, by B. S. Keirstead (Oxford, Basil Blackwell, 1953), pp. 57–8. This, no doubt, partly explains the pressure on, and development of, management accounting.

but items two, eight, nine and ten in Mr. May's list usually require more detailed statements than those customarily presented to shareholders in this country. There is one further use which has not been touched upon. I refer to the importance of published company accounts as source material for statistical and factual investigations in the field of applied economics, especially those which study the problems of business finance, taxation and the like. I believe that this utilization of published accounts is becoming more and more important, both for companies themselves and for the economic well-being of the nation as a whole.

The uses to which published accounts are put should have a bearing on their formal presentation.

7. In order to be useful published company accounts must be logical and clear. Good accounts are simple as well as 'true and fair'.

8. There are three serviceable ideas associated with the description of economic activity, which are relevant to accounting. The first, that of continuous flows of goods and services and of financial incomings and outgoings through time. The second, that of changes in stocks of possessions and financial claims over time. The third, that of stocks of possessions and financial claims at a moment of time. In general terms we may say that income is a flow and that capital is a stock. Accordingly, a profit and loss account is a flow account and a balance sheet is a stock account. A capital change account or a source and use of funds statement is a semi-flow account reconciled with stock changes.

9. The economic process is continuous through time, and therefore accounting theory prefers to think of an operating entity as continuous through time. Flow transactions can be given time dimensions which we call accounting periods, and in any survey of economic transactions time is clearly one of the fundamental variables. The importance of time has always been understood in the physical sciences, and as matter to inform our own subject, I give two quotations. One—'Since the essence of any physical problem is the observing and accounting for Nature's *changes*, of which any static condition is a limit rarely reached, time is the

fundamental variable for the physical sciences.'[1] Two—'Time implies—just the order in which we perceive events inevitably, as first recognized by Leibnitz. Experience, quantitative and qualitative, is always of such a sequence.'[2]

It is easy to see that an operating account covers a phase in a step-by-step analysis of the economic working of an entity. Inputs and outputs are flows which are going on more or less continuously, but an accounting presentation of activity engaged in for the use of shareholders is necessarily a static analysis after the events, and for stewardship reasons the time period adopted is relatively long term. We have to be unreal and assume that activity is annually, momentarily discontinuous. This is a reasonable way of looking at things when our main concern is with measures of disposable income, but it is quite inadequate for managing a company. Entrepreneurs must have information on what is really happening to the rates of flows of inputs and outputs, and the causes of changes, in order that their enterprises can be kept adaptable to changes. For this purpose the points of assumed discontinuity implicit in the time intervals of accounting periods must be brought as nëar to continuity as reason can contrive. Time differences *have* to be shortened; otherwise, sharp unpredictable variations in flows will not be recognized and dealt with.

Short period operating accounts are not necessary for publication to shareholders, but they are quite essential for those who conduct the company's business, for it is only through knowledge of the rate of changes in input and output flows that opinions on expectations can be formed. Changing flows of this order are not immediately visible in published annual accounts, and shareholders should never read more into them than they imply, e.g. without other evidence it should not be readily assumed that one year is necessarily a guide to another.

The profit and loss account of operating activity is a statement of aggregate flow transactions, and the time interval for which it is prepared governs its interpretation.

10. I pass now to some formal considerations affecting published

[1] *Time and Universe for the Scientific Conscience*, by Martin Johnson (Cambridge University Press, 1952), pp. 2–3. [2] *Ibid.*, p. 3.

company profit and loss accounts, and I begin with the legal constraints. I know that the provisions of the Companies Act, 1948, are more than familiar to you all, nevertheless I think it is instructive to re-examine them, more especially as I want to work them into a set of principles. The first point to notice is that in the main the Companies Act, 1948, concentrates upon disclosure provisions; it only deals with form and measurement in a very indirect kind of way. Thus: 'Every profit and loss account of a company shall give a true and fair view of the profit or loss of the company for the financial year' (S. 149(1)). The expression 'true and fair' has a note of tautology about it, but no doubt its meaning is clear for everyday understanding. Leaving on one side the explanatory matters required to be stated by way of a note to the profit and loss account, and those special issues which affect a consolidated profit and loss account, the statutory disclosure requirements may be shortly summarized as the following items:

i. Provision for depreciation, renewals or diminution in value of fixed assets.
ii. Interest on debentures and other fixed loans.
iii. Income tax and other taxation on profits.
iv. Provisions for redemption of share capital, and for redemption of loans.
v. Material transfers to, or withdrawals from, reserves.
vi. Material transfers to, or withdrawals from, provisions.
vii. Income from investments, distinguishing between trade and other investments.
viii. Dividends paid and proposed.
ix. Directors' emoluments.
x. Directors' pensions.
xi. Compensation to directors for loss of office.
xii. Auditors' remuneration (if not fixed by the company in general meeting).[1]

[1] Eighth Schedule, 12 and 13, and Section 196, Companies Act, 1948. See also the following detailed references: *Design of Accounts*, pp. 48–65 (Oxford University Press, third edition 1949; second impression, 1956); *The Measurement of Profit* (Oxford University Press, first edition, 1949; second impression, 1953); pp. 44–5; *Four Essays in Accounting Theory* (Oxford University Press, 1953), pp. 28–9.

11. I think it is clear that many of these items are unlike in character, and the first task is to set them within classifications appropriate to the nature of the transactions they represent, and those concepts which order the principles of accounting design. 'The amount charged to revenue by way of provision for depreciation, renewals or diminution in value of fixed assets' is ordinarily an imputed transaction *before* arriving at opcrating profit. I am always a little puzzled at this disclosure and I sometimes doubt whether it is particularly informative as the bare statement of an amount divorced from a full account of operating activity, more especially since, if not otherwise shown, a note on the profit and loss account is wanted in the following circumstances, and to the effect that—'If depreciation or replacement of fixed assets is provided for by some method other than a depreciation charge or provision for renewals, or is not provided for, the method by which it is provided for or the fact that it is not provided for, as the case may be.'[1] May be there *is* some merit in knowing the magnitude of an imputed charge, about which there is bound to be some uncertainty, in relation to a more certain gross measure of profit; but if this is so, the latter figure should be plainly asked for, which at present it is not, and taking all in all, it is surely the net measure which is really significant, i.e. the operating profit. Although I do not propose to go into measurement problems here, there are a few enlightened companies which provide for depreciation on the basis of the replacement values of fixed assets in use at the terminal date of accounts. As a consequence, there can be little question that the users of published company accounts should be told whether the charge made for depreciation before arriving at operating profit is an allocation of historical costs, or whether it is based on replacement values, and in the latter case there is obvious merit in disclosing the price change element.

12. This seems the place to make a brief mention of the relevance of some recent ideas on the financial effects of provisions for depreciation, especially when based on replacement values. Expanding enterprises tend to accumulate expanding depreciation funds because of natural delays, or time lags, in actual replacements.

[1] Eighth Schedule, 14.

As is well known to bankers and others, such funds are factors in promoting financial independence, and because of this, voices are raised in favour of discounted provisions. I think it is well to be clear on this. An imputed charge for depreciation pure and simple, even though it is based on current asset values at the terminal date of accounts, is nothing more than a conjoined measure of user cost and deterioration through time. As such it immediately replaces original capital resources in some other form; a form which may well be temporarily financial in character. Nevertheless, it is still a part of the original resources, and apart from the necessities of an expanding working capital, it should be kept invested in revenue earning assets, whether real or financial. (Preferably real when money values are falling.) Hence, the utilization of depreciation funds is merely a means of keeping original capital resources invested, and the revenue earned from the utilization of those funds is, at all times, part of the total income of the enterprise. It is *not* a prospect to be taken into account in assessing periodical so-called *ex-ante* fixed asset replacement provisions.

13. Whilst we are on this subject of depreciation funds, I think we should just notice some balance sheet requirements of the Companies Act, 1948. Thus:

The method of arriving at the amount of any fixed asset shall . . . be to take the difference between—

(*a*) its cost or, if it stands in the company's books at a valuation, the amount of the valuation; and

(*b*) the aggregate amount provided or written off since the date of acquisition or valuation, as the case may be, for depreciation or diminution in value;

and again:

For the assets under each heading . . . there shall be shown—

(*a*) the aggregate of the amounts referred to in paragraph (*a*)—(above) . . . and

(*b*) the aggregate of the amounts referred to in paragraph (*b*)—(above).[1]

[1] Eighth Schedule, 5.

This means that accumulated depreciation provisions are separately disclosed for classified fixed assets. I have often wondered what this particular disclosure had to tell recipients of published company accounts, but presumably it is meant as a measure of that part of currently operating assets which has been used up. It may be questioned how far the disclosure of such an aggregate for the assets under each heading is useful for a proper understanding of its adequacy, since in fact we know nothing about the age composition of the assets.

14. In the profit and loss disclosure requirement which we have been mainly examining in the last few paragraphs, there is a reference to the 'diminution in value of fixed assets', and the question immediately presents itself; diminution in value, from what cause? Presumably the statutory reference is related to obsolescence, but since it is our concern to classify the nature of the imputed charge, we ought to ask ourselves whether obsolescence is wholly a charge before arriving at operating profit, or whether it has some of the characteristics of a capital loss. No doubt it is expedient to treat a 'provision for depreciation, renewals, or diminution in value of fixed assets' as an amount to be *charged to revenue*, thereby bringing an aggregate within the disclosure requirement of the statute, but in so far as there is any element of capital loss, it should be assigned, theoretically, to a capital change account. Perhaps we should look at this question a little more deeply.

15. The features of a capital loss, associated with a fixed asset, may be thought of in the following terms:

(*a*) Realization: The loss should be realized, or if unrealized in the sense that there has been no exchange transaction, the fixed asset source of the loss should be without value, and incapable of further use.

(*b*) Irregularity: The loss should be unforeseen and unexpected, uncertain and fortuitous, and therefore unallowed for.

It is sometimes said that obsolescence is always unforeseeable, but experience does not entirely support this view. Technological development in a quickly changing industry is to some extent expected, and in so far as this expectation can be imputed in accounting provisions, the resulting charges are properly treated as revenue inputs. In theory, at least, an unexpected loss due, for example, to sudden technological change should be treated as a capital loss, and disclosed in a capital change account. We shall have more to say about this account later. In the meantime, however, we should remark that the line of demarcation is not always apparent. Sometimes it is blurred and grey, in which case practice and common sense would have the charge against income.

16. The next disclosure requirement affecting the profit and loss account need not detain us for long. I refer to the fact that there shall be shown 'the amount of the interest on the company's debentures and other fixed loans'. This is plainly to be classified as a financial outgoing before deriving the total income of the company.

17. We pass on to the separate disclosure of 'the amount of the charge for United Kingdom income tax and other United Kingdom taxation on profits, including, where practicable, as United Kingdom income tax any taxation imposed elsewhere to the extent of the relief, if any, from United Kingdom income tax and distinguishing where practicable between income tax and other taxation'. The basis on which the charge for United Kingdom income tax is computed is also required to be stated by way of a note to the profit and loss account, if not otherwise shown. These taxation disclosures fall within the category of income transfers, because in the aggregate they represent a part of the company's income over which it has no outlay decision. In effect, this part of its income is sooner or later transferred to the central government by way of the Inland Revenue machinery for assessment and collection. Companies are comparatively easy to deal with when it comes to the assessment and collection of taxes, and so we find them subject to two taxes, an income tax, and a profits tax. It is right that they should be noted separately because the basis of assessment is not the same in both cases. There is also the added complication of a distribution tax within the profits tax. A recent correspondent in *Accountancy* suggested that the distribution profits tax applicable

to both Preference and Ordinary dividends should be shown as inset additions to the respective net amounts of those dividends. Whilst I agreed with what he said, I did not like the confusion in formal principles which resulted. Taxation and dividends are both transfers of income, but they are very different in character. The amount of a dividend is within a company's decisions, whereas the greater part of the amount of taxation is not. I, therefore, prefer to see an aggregate for all taxation disclosed as a separate transfer of income in a company's published profit and loss account, although this need not hinder any detailed showing of its make-up.

18. The next item in our list of legal constraints which concerns the profit and loss account requires the statement of 'the amounts respectively provided for redemption of share capital and for redemption of loans'. In our student days these entries seemed to have puzzling traits, but they are really only appropriations out of income to reserve funds. Nevertheless, it is important to notice that whereas in the course of events an amount provided for redemption of share capital will ordinarily acquire the status of a *capital* reserve, an amount provided for redemption of loans is not necessarily in the same class; it could very well be a revenue reserve. Nevertheless, both amounts should be included in those accounts which show the sources, earmarkings and utilization of funds, i.e. the transfers to and from retained income, and the capital changes. The separate showing of 'the amount, if material, set aside or proposed to be set aside to, or withdrawn from, reserves' falls into place in much the same way. Such an amount is either a transfer from, or to, retained income.

19. And now we come to items of difficulty. How should we classify 'the amount, if material, set aside to provisions other than provisions for depreciation, renewals or diminution in value of assets or, as the case may be, the amount, if material, withdrawn from such provisions and not applied for the purposes thereof'? One of the troubles with a provision is that it is supposed to be incapable of determination with substantial accuracy, and cannot, therefore, be treated as a straightforward accrual. Nevertheless, if it is associated with operating activity in the shape of some sort

of liability attaching to goods and services, however inaccurately determined, it must have the character of an outgoing to be charged before the ascertainment of operating profit. An amount withdrawn from provisions because it is no longer required, seems to have much the same status as any adjustment to the profit measures of prior years. I am, therefore, tempted to regard a withdrawal from provisions on much the same basis as a withdrawal from reserves, by treating it as a transfer to the retained income of the period within the statement of sources, earmarkings and utilization of funds.

20. The item—income from investments—is a financial incoming to be generally dealt with as financial rather than operating income, although we should notice the obvious relevance of the requirement to distinguish between trade and other investments. Dividends paid and proposed, as we have seen, are in the category of income transfers, and should be treated as such.

21. The four remaining profit and loss disclosure items: namely those which relate to directors' emoluments, directors' pensions, compensation to directors for loss of office, and auditors' remuneration, do not call for extensive classification comments. Directors' emoluments, directors' pensions, and the relatively minor item of auditors' remuneration (if not fixed by the company in general meeting), have the characteristics of charges to revenue before the ascertainment of operating profit. Presumably the disclosure emphasis on outgoings to directors is politic, but I sometimes wonder if the statement of these aggregates in relation to some indeterminate figure of profit, is not out of proportion. I should much prefer to see them dealt with as part of the more significant aggregate for administration and management expenses, or with rather more justification, the total input allocations for labour and capital.[1] Although most companies may prefer to regard compensation paid to directors for loss of office as a current operating charge to revenue, it does have the nature of an exceptional or non-recurrent transaction, and as such should be stated after the normal measure of operating profit, but before the measurement

[1] Cf. the account for operating activity in *Four Essays in Accounting Theory* (Oxford University Press, 1953), p. 41.

of total income, along with transactions of a sort not usually undertaken by the company.

22. Readers of *Accounting Research* may remember that about a year or so ago, I gave a simple analysis of formal accounting on the following lines.[1]

I. CURRENT

i. Operating activity	Real
ii. Income	Real
	± Financial items
	± Transfers
	= Disposable income
iii. Outlay	Disposable income
	= Consumption[2]
	+ Saving

II. SOURCE AND USE OF FUNDS (CAPITAL CHANGES)

i. Saving and internal operating provisions.
ii. Real asset formation.
iii. Valuation changes.
iv. Financial incomings and outgoings, and changes in monetary claims.

(The ultimate resolution of the accounting identity—
Saving=Investment.)

III. CAPITAL

Real wealth and net monetary claims.

It seems to me that this arrangement establishes a basic framework for the ideas we have been discussing in this lecture.

23. Accordingly, I set out below a plan of accounts, set to this framework, which I should regard as the most desirable statement of the permissible minimum.

[1] 'Design for the Accounts of Society', *Accounting Research*, Vol. 3, No. 1 January, 1952, pp. 18–19 (Cambridge University Press).

[2] This item is not relevant in public company accounting.

PROFIT AND LOSS ACCOUNT

I. PROVISION FOR DEPRECIATION, renewals or diminution in value of fixed assets, indicating where relevant:			I. PROFIT before disclosed charges	x
i. Cost allocation ...	x			
ii. Price change adjustment	x			
		x		
II. PROVISIONS to meet liabilities for goods and services		x		
III. DIRECTORS' EMOLUMENTS		x		
IV. DIRECTORS' OR PAST DIRECTORS' PENSIONS ...		x		
V. AUDITORS' REMUNERATION —if not fixed by the company in general meeting		x		
VI. OPERATING PROFIT ...		x		
		x		x

I. COMPENSATION TO DIRECTORS for loss of office ...	x	I. OPERATING PROFIT ...	x
II. TRANSACTIONS of a sort not usually undertaken ...	x	II. TRANSACTIONS of a sort not usually undertaken ...	x
III. INTEREST on the company's debentures and other fixed loans (before income tax)	x	III. INCOME FROM INVESTMENTS (before income tax and suitably analysed) ...	x
IV. INCOME	x		
	x		x

PROFIT AND LOSS ACCOUNT—*continued*

I. UNITED KINGDOM income tax and other United Kingdom taxation on profits (detailed)			I. INCOME		x
i. Actual basis	x				
ii. Deferred basis... ...	x				
	—	x			
II. DIVIDENDS paid and proposed (before income tax)		x			
		—			
INCOME TRANSFERS ...		x			
III. RETAINED INCOME ...		x			
		—			—
		x			x
		=			=

SOURCES, EARMARKINGS AND UTILIZATION OF FUNDS

I. ADJUSTMENTS to past income measures ...	x		I. RETAINED INCOME ...	x	
II. ADJUSTMENTS to past taxation transfers	x		II. ADJUSTMENTS to past income measures, e.g. withdrawals from provisions	x	
	—	x		—	x
III. AMOUNTS respectively provided for redemption of share capital and loans ...	x		III. WITHDRAWALS FROM RESERVES		x
IV. TRANSFERS TO RESERVES ...	x				
	—	x			
V. REPORTED INCREASE in undistributed income ...		x			
		—			—
		x			x
		=			=

SOURCES, EARMARKINGS AND UTILIZATION OF FUNDS
—continued

I. NET EXPENDITURE ON:
- i. Tangible fixed assets x
- ii. Intangible fixed assets x

— x

II. INCREASE (or decrease*) in deferred expenditure x

III. INCREASE (or decrease*) in total inventories ... x

— x

IV. INCREASE (or decrease*) in security investments x

V. LONG-TERM LENDING (new—positive, repaid negative) x

VI. CAPITAL LOSSES (e.g. Unforeseen obsolescence) x

— x

VII. CHANGES IN CURRENT ASSET CLAIMS (increases —positive, decreases— negative)
- i. Customers' credit x
- ii. Unexpired claims ... x

— x

VIII. INCREASE IN MONETARY BALANCES x

— x

—

x

═

* Negative

I. REPORTED INCREASE in undistributed income x

II. EARMARKED INCOME (redemptions and reserves) x

— x

III. PROVISION FOR DEPRECIATION
- i. Cost allocation ... x
- ii. Price Change adjustment* x

— x

IV. INVENTORY price change adjustment* x

— x

V. CAPITAL (new—positive, repaid—negative) ... x

VI. LONG-TERM BORROWING (new—positive, repaid —negative) x

VII. CAPITAL GAINS x

— x

VIII. CHANGES IN CURRENT LIABILITY CLAIMS (Increases—positive, decreases—negative)
- i. Short term borrowing x
- ii. Suppliers' credit ... x
- iii. Accruals x
- iv. Dividend and interest claims x
- v. Current tax liabilities x

— x

IX. DECREASE IN MONETARY BALANCES (Bank, cash and tax reserve certificates) ... x

X. CHANGES IN PROVISIONS (Increases—positive, decreases—negative) x

XI. CHANGES IN DEFERRED LIABILITIES (e.g. taxation), (Increases—positive, decreases—negative) x

— x

—

x

═

* Increase positive, or decrease negative

Note: In those cases where valuation adjustments have been taken to account, the capital adjustment will be credited and the asset adjustment debited, in the immediately preceding account. (Increases—positive, decreases—negative.)

BALANCE SHEET

I. Authorised Capital (detailed) —

II. Issued Capital and Capital Reserves
- i. Issued (detailed) ... x
- ii. Capital redemption reserve fund ... x
- iii. Premium accounts ... x
- iv. Capital reserves ... x

— x

III. Revenue Reserves and Retained Income
- i. Revenue reserves x
- ii. Undistributed income x

— x

IV. Price Change Adjustments
- i. Depreciation ... x
- ii. Inventories ... x

— x

— x

V. Long-term Liability Claims (with a separate disclosure indication of those which are secured) x

VI. Provisions x

VII. Current Liability Claims (with a separate disclosure indication of those which are secured)
- i. Short-term borrowing x
- ii. Creditors and accrued expenses ... x
- iii. Current tax liabilities... x
- iv. Proposed dividends x

— x

VIII. Deferred Liabilities ... x

—

x

I. Fixed Assets (with a disclosure of the basis of valuation)
- i. Real or physical
  - 1. Structures ... x
    Minus accumulated depreciation x
    — x
  - 2. Equipment ... x
    Minus accumulated depreciation x
    — x
- ii. Deferred expenditure benefiting the activities of future accounting periods x
- iii. Standard (normal or base) inventories x
- iv. Intangible ... x

— x

II. Long-term Asset Claims
- i. Investments (with a separate disclosure of trade, quoted and unquoted investments) ... x
- ii. Lending (with a separate disclosure of loans to employees, directors or officers) x

— x

III. Current Asset Claims
- i. Excess over standard inventories (with a disclosure of the basis of valuation) x
- ii. Debtors and unexpired payments ... x
- iii. Monetary balances x

— x

—

x

24. From this plan of accounts for public companies, I derive the following formal principles:

The profit and loss account should be formulated to reveal:

i. The operating profit of the period.
ii. The financial income and transactions of a kind not usually undertaken.
iii. The total income of the period.
iv. The transfers out of total income.
v. The retained income of the period.

Part I of the account for sources, earmarkings, and utilization of funds should be designed to give a clear indication of:

i. The appropriation of the retained income of the period.
ii. Adjustments to past profit and loss account measures.
iii. Withdrawals from reserves.
iv. The reported increase in undistributed income.

Part II of the same account should be framed to show capital changes, in particular:

i. The saving of the period, depreciation and gross asset formation.
ii. Changes in money capital and long term claims; capital gains and losses.
iii. The reconciling changes in current claims and monetary balances, provisions and deferred liabilities.

The balance sheet should be designed to show:

I. i. Money capital and non-distributable resources.
ii. Saved income.
iii. Price change adjustments.
iv. Capital employed.
v. Long term liability claims.
vi. Provisions.
vii. Current liability claims.
viii. Deferred liabilities.

II. i. Fixed assets: real or physical, deferred expenditure, standard inventories and intangible items.
ii. Long term asset claims.
iii. Current asset claims.

25. Those of you who have read my *Four Essays in Accounting Theory*[1] will know that I prefer an openly displayed operating account, but so far the Companies Acts have not lent support to this view. In effect, the Companies Act of 1948 calls for an appropriation account with some categories that do not belong there.

26. Part II of the account for sources, earmarkings and utilization of funds is a capital change account, and I shall discuss its implications in a later lecture.

The capital change account is important for a company's proper understanding of its own affairs, for example, to indicate the financial limits on *real* investment, or the financial implications of changing tax reserves. It also serves such factual inquiries over a wide area, as seek to provide information for the implementation of reasonable fiscal policies. I shall continue to press for its permanent place in public company accounting.

27. I have no great reason to criticize the balance sheet disclosure requirements of the Companies Act, 1948, except to say that I do regard the distinction between the real and the financial, as quite fundamental. I have given my reasons for treating standard inventories as fixed assets in *Four Essays in Accounting Theory*. Therefore, I cannot but regard inventory profits and losses as capital changes. After all, no accountant would think of treating a profit or loss on the re-valuation of structures or equipment as part of operating profit. For the rest, a balance sheet should always give a plain indication of non-distributable resources, and of distributable resources.

28. One last general comment. Such notes as are required should be few, significant and material and they should never be allowed to disturb the formal and logical presentation of the accounts themselves.

[1] Oxford University Press, 1953.

3

ACCOUNTING DYNAMICS—I

A research lecture given at Incorporated Accountants Hall, London, on 30th March, 1954

'. . . collecting facts recedes before the task of the intellectual digestion of these facts and of developing their implications.'

SCHUMPETER.[1]

'Time itself is defined in terms of change.'

AQUINAS.[2]

'In truth we know nothing unerringly, but only as it changes according to the disposition of our body, and of the things that enter into it and impinge on it.'

DEMOCRITUS. (D.fr. 9).[3]

1. In this lecture, of necessity heavily documented, we shall begin to deal with the analysis and study of changes in accounting aggregates. Accounting dynamics can and should be looked upon as part of the general interpretation of accounts. It is not an entirely new study. The familiar comparison of standard costs with actual costs, inasmuch as it concentrates upon an understanding of differences, is a beginning in the dynamic approach to accounting data. Our primary purpose then is to consider those forms of differential accounts which promote business adaptability to change.

2. Before starting on this line, however, we should recall one or two fundamental conceptions which have their origin in the very nature and purpose of the accounting exercise. Thus, the exercise itself is a means of systematizing economic transactions to help us to understand the workings of those agents in society which create incomes, spend incomes, and add to or subtract from wealth.

[1] Essay on Eugen von Böhm-Bawerk, in *Ten Great Economists*, by Joseph A. Schumpeter (George Allen & Unwin Ltd., 1952), p. 157.

[2] *Philosophical Texts*, selected and translated by Thomas Gilby, No. 131 (Oxford University Press, 1951).

[3] This quotation has been taken from Professor Schrödinger's Shearman Lectures, delivered at University College, London, in May, 1948, which are now published under the title *Nature and the Greeks* (Cambridge University Press, 1954). Professor Schrödinger remarks that the translations of the fragments of Democritus follow Cyril Bailey. (See p. 87.)

By planned arrangements of aggregates it unifies a great number of diverse transactions, and thereby succinctly explains both the utilization of, and state of, resources, which assists those who have to make decisions about economic activities and their financial implications.

3. We know that it is only prudent to keep a watch over resources and their disposition, and especially of changes in those resources through time. If they are to be preserved and extended then it is imperative to keep under view the course of an entity's affairs, as was recognized a long time ago. The following quotation taken from an article on *Accountantship* in *The Universal Dictionary of Trade and Commerce*, translated from the French of Monsieur Savary 'with large additions and improvements' by Malachy Postlethwayt (First Edition 1751), although written in the style, and within the social climate of its day, is not without point in the context of our present inquiry.

> And as it becomes all persons of the greater distinction to take due care of their estates; so nothing perhaps can have a happier tendency to that end, than a knowledge in the art of debtor and creditor, as well as that of numbers. For *merchants accounts*, says Mr. Locke, 'though a science not likely to help a gentleman to get an estate, yet possibly there is not anything of more use and efficacy to make him preserve the estate he has. *'Tis seldom observed that he who keeps an account of his income and expense, and thereby has constantly under view the course of his domestic affairs, lets them run to ruin.* And I doubt not but many a man gets behind before he is aware, or runs farther on when he is once in, for want of his care, or the skill to do it. I would therefore advise all gentlemen to learn perfectly *merchants accounts*, and not to think it a skill that belongs not to them, because it has received its name and has been chiefly practised by men of traffic.'[1]

4. We also know that in accounting the monetary unit is the conventional basis of record and measurement because of its convenience as a medium of exchange, as a store of value and as a standard of value. It has always endeared itself to recorders of transactions as purporting to be a means of bringing together the

[1] Italics mine. I owe this quotation to Mr. T. R. Johnston, a Cambridge research student.

valences of unlike things. As Adam Smith observed: 'Money has become in all civilized nations the universal instrument of commerce, by the intervention of which goods of all kinds are bought and sold, or exchanged for one another.'[1] Nevertheless, although money continues to regulate the *business* of everyday life, interpretations based on changes in money measures have their pitfalls, and there is here a difficult field for accounting researchers to roam in; we can only hope to touch upon it in this discussion. For example, in a recent review of *Four Essays in Accounting Theory*,[2] Professor Stone referred to the preliminary report on the *Measurement of Productive Efficiency* prepared by a sub-committee of the Incorporated Accountants' Research Committee in 1951, and the several possible measures of productivity in financial and related physical terms which were there set out. He said that:

'While it would undoubtedly be useful to have measures of the variables which enter into these relationships, it may be doubted whether this information would in fact provide either a general measure of changes in productivity or a means of ascribing changes, if they could be ascertained, to the various contributing factors. Productivity changes, if the volume of net output (or value added or processing) changes in relation to the volume of factors of production employed in the process. A measure of the volume of net output involves, in virtually every practical case, an index number problem and also difficulties of determining appropriate units in which to measure the constituent quantities. It seems probable that in many cases these difficulties can be overcome. A more searching question is the provision of quantity measures of factor inputs. One of these, labour employed, seems to offer a relatively easy target and so many empirical measures are found of labour productivity. It would appear, however, that . . . other factor inputs should be treated in a similar way to labour and it is not at all clear how this is to be done. For it implies not merely that accounts show transactions grouped into meaningful categories . . . but also that operationally significant measures of quantity and unit price be associated with these transactions and especially, since this is the main difficulty, with

[1] *The Wealth of Nations*—Everyman Edition, Vol. 1, p. 24.

[2] Published for the Incorporated Accountants' Research Committee by the Oxford University Press in 1953.

purchases of factor services. Here we still seem to be pretty much in the dark.'[1]

This means that when it comes to a significant understanding of changes in accounting aggregate categories in any real sense, then we are still toying around with a highly sensitive monetary unit of measure which is acutely affected by purely financial considerations. At the financial perimeter of economic activity it tells the story well enough, but it leaves us with indeterminate interpretations of some essential relationships at the heart of the matter. Real and financial relationships reside in two very different departments of accounting knowledge, and there is much to be done before we reach daylight in the first branch. Nevertheless, the problem must be faced. Professor Stone would like to see a concrete example of how properly organized data can assist in the solution of this kind of problem. He says that: 'In a difficult matter of this kind, detailed empirical research on a small number of specific cases for which the fullest information can be obtained would seem the best way of sorting out the real from the imaginary problems.' In due time we had better take the hint, but we should not overlook the attention which some cost accountants have already given to specific engineering production functions.

5. So much by way of introduction to some of the problems inherent in change relationships, but we have yet to introduce some further reflections on the nature of accounting changes, and we must reach clear ideas about the form and contents of change accounts before we can seriously contemplate a dynamic approach to the theory of accounting. A long task lies ahead of us, yet it is important to call to mind that accounting probably started as a means of taking stock of *changes in possessions*, which, apart from mere transfers of wealth, were later revealed as differences between income and spending. These early ideas still have significance as can be seen from a study of the primary functions of accounts. In an earlier lecture I listed six functions based on a few fundamental concepts, one of which was specifically related to

[1] *Accounting Research*, Vol. 4, No. 4, October 1953, p. 401.

a portrayal of the uses to which saving had been put and the measurement of capital changes over time. It appeared among these functions because of the importance of saving and investment as a cardinal identity in the design of accounts. It now seems to me that if we are to establish any kind of change relationships in accounting then we must also find a place for the measurement of changes in the make-up of periodic incomes as an additional function of accounts, and later on in this discussion we shall have to give some close attention to the form and contents of an income change account.

6. Since we are embarking on a difficult and uncertain extension of accounting ideas, we should perhaps remind ourselves that on the practical plane of expediency, modern accounting practice owes its importance to its close attachment to the needs of business enterprise. Profits or enterprise income, and financial solvency are major considerations in the conduct of any business. Profits are taxed, part distributed, and part saved, so that a fair accounting measure over time is a matter of consequence to all entrepreneurs. Apart from taxation, undistributed profits have become important indicators of the stabilizing and developing powers of business enterprises. The *continuing* ability to earn profits is still regarded as a criterion of effectiveness and a guarantor of capital values. It is important to recognize that this *continuing* ability to earn profits very largely depends upon business adaptability to change both on income and capital accounts, whether real or financial.

7. Again, it seems that there is much justification for this emphasis on profits. Little has observed that:

In contrast to any so-called consumers'-surplus criterion, profitability really is a criterion. If the aim is profits, and an enterprise is started with that in view, then we can, at least, tell whether its objective was achieved. Profitability is easy to test, and it is possible to gain experience in profit estimation. There remains the fact that the objective is not 'ideal', and also the fact that considerable monopoly power may have to be wielded in order to obtain the profit. This is not, in itself, an objection, because one can also estimate, and gain experience in estimating, the profit or loss that would accrue as a result of making the change and adopting a certain pricing policy. In extreme cases, as where the pricing policy is to charge nothing, then, of course, any such objective criterion ceases to be possible. We do not . . . wish to go into more practical matters, but merely to point out that if profitability (with or without certain conditions imposed) is abandoned, as a criterion for making finite changes, then there is no definite, generally applicable, rule which can replace it.[1]

8. Thus, accountants have a major interest in the measurement of profit or enterprise income, and although we may appear to be harking back on to an old theme, it is not surprising that periodic income is one of the conceptual sources for the derivation of accounting principles. These principles must always constitute the starting point from which we go forward to new developments, and all the way through our research work we shall find ourselves continually returning to them. Moreover, it is especially necessary to remind those who practice accounting that first principles *are* important because they lend significance to a subject and give it a place in the broader regions of human thought and action. We may perhaps turn aside to remark that there can be little question that accounting ought to have such a place. Kuznets has said that:

The spread of the industrial system to an increasing number of countries, and its progressively deeper penetration into the fabric of social life, mean a growing supply of statistics of steadily improving quality and increasing wealth of detail. This trend is due to a variety of factors, among which are the growing measurability and practice of accounting in everyday life. . . . The supply of *economic* statistics has been particularly enriched because of the increasing value that society places upon performance in the field of economic attainment. . . . [2]

So far as the individual entity is concerned, efficient performance, as we have said, is largely a matter of adaptability to change, and in recognizing the concepts of income and capital as fundamental to the practice of accounting, we should also see that there are possibilities in a 'marginal' approach which studies

[1] *A Critique of Welfare Economics*, by I. M. D. Little (Oxford, Clarendon Press, 1950), p. 178.

[2] 'Statistical Trends and Historical Changes', by Simon Kuznets. *The Economic History Review*, Second Series, Vol. III, No. 3, 1951 (Cambridge University Press).

changes in the make-up of periodic incomes, capital changes, and their likely inter-relation, because it is by an understanding of these matters that decay may be arrested, and performance maintained.

9. In the previous lecture we dealt with the distinction between flows and stocks, and in general terms we described income as a flow and capital as a stock. It follows from this that capital changes are represented by variations in stocks of possessions and financial claims, while income changes are brought about by alterations in flow transactions. Since the economic process is continuous through time, flow transactions go on more or less continuously. Accordingly, the important thing to notice is what is happening to the rates of flows of inputs and outputs which make up income generation, and to find this out *as it goes on under our gaze.* To do this, 'the points of assumed discontinuity implicit in the time intervals of accounting periods must be brought as near to continuity' as can be arranged, so that we learn something about the variability which a continuous process is undergoing. As we commented in the previous lecture, 'time differences *have* to be shortened; otherwise, sharp unpredictable variations in flows will not be recognized and dealt with'. Plainly, we must know something about the behaviour of short-term flow changes because they are the ones which must be counteracted when they go well out of the line of generally expected trends. This, then, suggests the method of attack when we come to deal with income changes.

10. We may suppose that in a world of continual economic change our economist friends would claim they had more analytical tools available for the propagation of dynamic theories than any manipulated patterns of account would be likely to reveal. But there is a strange warning from Schumpeter which ought to be emphasized, and which bears upon the view that far more can be done with the aid of accounting forms than is commonly supposed. He said that:

Concepts imply *relations* and since theory, so far as it consists in setting up rational schemata, is essentially a theory of an economic calculus, we may, instead of saying that the Walrasian system presupposes the solution of a problem of conceptualization, also say that it presupposes a schema of economic accounting. We know from experience, old and recent, that this conceptualization of schema of accounting centres in the themes of capital values and income values. This is why Walras included in his *Eléments d'Economie Politique Pure* a few paragraphs that might have been entitled: elementary principles of accounting. And this is also why Irving Fisher supplemented the *Investigations* by a volume on the *Nature of Capital and Income*. In the first place, Fisher accomplished a task that was long overdue. I do not know whether others are as impressed as I am by the historical fact that economists habitually neglect to avail themselves of obvious opportunities and to take the obvious line. The fate of D. Bernoulli's suggestive tract is a case in point. Economists' failure to join forces with engineers is another. But nothing is more illustrative of that attitude than is the neglect by nineteenth-century economists of the opportunities to learn from accounting and actuarial practice and in turn to try to rationalize it from the standpoint of economic theory. Attempts to do both are of comparatively recent origin and the more important of them, though no doubt subconsciously, follow Fisher's example. The response from accountants was only in part favourable, Professor Canning's work being the outstanding instance.[1]

For us, of course, there is a sting in the tail.

11. I am so concerned to establish the métier of accounting and to counter the last animadversion, that I propose, with your leave, to deflect the present course of argument and make a point. In a recent thesis I have sought to assert a pure theory of accounting which seeks to apply universal concepts of structure, form and measurement to any and every economic activity which requires to be viewed by means of accounts. In short, an invariant pattern exemplifying such a view of economic activity as points to an effective use of resources.[2] Is this so far different in conception from the schema brought out by Schumpeter when writing on Marshall? Thus:

The discovery that there is such a thing as a general method of economic analysis, or to put it differently, that as far as the logic of their

[1] *Ten Great Economists*, by Joseph A. Schumpeter (George Allen & Unwin Ltd., London, 1952), pp. 228–9.

[2] *Four Essays in Accounting Theory* (Oxford University Press, 1953).

procedure is concerned, economists, whether dealing with international trade or with unemployment or with profits or with money or whatnot, are always applying substantially the same schema that is invariant to the particular subject matter in hand . . . this discovery was not his. Nor was it the discovery of the group of economists of which he was so outstanding a member. In order to satisfy ourselves that this truth must have been known, at least from the Physiocrats on, to all economists that knew their business, we need only look at Ricardo's work. The first chapter, supplemented by the second, is obviously a blue-print of such an 'engine for the discovery of concrete truth', and the rest of Ricardo's chapters is nothing but a series of experiments in the application of that blue-print. But no economist before Marshall ever grasped the meaning of this so fully, preached it so energetically, acted upon it so consistently . . . Marshall's historic-philosophical culture tells on almost every page.[1]

Accounting research is discovering the universals in what is properly its own blue-print.

12. Or, yet again, we might listen to Professor Robbins.

In France, in the hands of Cantillon and the Physiocrats, and in Britain, in the hands of the Scotch Philosophers, economics had passed from a series of *ad hoc* inquiries to an analysis of general interconnections. It appealed to general uniformities rather than particular instances. It presented principles of explanation applicable to a wide variety of circumstances. In short, it had assumed the form and the objectives of a science in the Kantian sense. It was on this body of knowledge, at least in part, that the English Classical Economists professed to base their theory of policy. And it is this claim which is one of the chief characteristics distinguishing them from most other schools.[2]

As economic theory has been built up from a few ideas based on general uniformities, so I think accounting theory is beginning to reveal itself, for at bottom both theories have a logical basis in the same select concepts. But to return to the main stream of the present argument, it is from the formal pattern grounded on select concepts, which is at the heart of accounting practice, that we

[1] *Ten Great Economists*, by Joseph A. Schumpeter (George Allen & Unwin Ltd., London, 1952), pp. 101–2.

[2] *The Theory of Economic Policy in English Classical Political Economy*, by Lionel Robbins (Macmillan, 1952), p. 172.

should look for 'change' relationships, and we should, therefore, expect any presentations of 'change' accounts to conform in principle with that invariant design which is implicit in the main accounts themselves.

13. Change itself has become a condition of man's life. Dr. J. R. Oppenheimer recently opened his Reith lectures on 'Science and the Common Understanding' with the simple statement that: 'Science has changed the conditions of man's life. . . . It has altered the communities in which we live and cherish, learn and act. It has made change itself the condition of man's life.' It has plainly made change a condition of economic activity and has thereby brought it within the immediate concern of accountants, for accounting is taken up with the analysis and summary presentation of sequential economic data in order that we may have a better understanding of the course of economic events as they affect the selected entity for whom we choose to account. Indeed, those requirements of the Companies Act, 1948, which call for comparative figures in a sense constitute a recognition of the importance of change.

14. For our purposes, I think that if they can be suitably devised, accounting models in the form of change accounts are to be preferred to some of those mathematical models which econometricians have experimented with in developing economic dynamics. I particularly want to make it clear that I only say this in the present context for the utilitarian reason that business men are likely to be more familiar with accounting designs and, therefore, better able to understand their purport. Accounts, as we know them, can be thought of as special frameworks for the positioning of financial statistics, and perhaps Kuznets was pondering something of the kind, though from a different point of view, when he said that:

The moral is not, of course, that we should forbear from the use of statistical data. On the contrary, their peculiar advantage makes them an extremely important type of primary information, not equalled or replaceable by other types of data. Their use should be more widespread and intensive than heretofore—but divorced from the rather mechanistic approach that employs mathematical models as hasty simulacra of controlled experimental situations (which they are not), and wedded to full cognisance of the variety and mutability of historical changes in human society.[1]

15. I think it well to make it clear, however, that the kind of changes we shall be thinking about in these lectures are those which happen to the individual firm, and particularly those which are involuntary. The object of management accounting should be the study of those economic changes which affect the firm. Such changes do *not* necessarily follow the same trends as those with which econometricians have been mainly concerned in their macrocosms. Thus, although it may be possible to give a likely estimate of the general aggregate demand for the products of a particular industry, nevertheless, there can still be substantial variability between firms. There are better prediction possibilities when we are dealing with large aggregates because of the offsetting of errors of detail. Involuntary changes which are liable to affect individual firms must be detected as and when they arise, and I suggest that a sensitive vehicle for doing this should have the form of a short period change account. There is also a further point which Stone has mentioned in his survey of Model Building and the Social Accounts. 'Thus, if an input-output model is used to review the implications of an expected change in final demand it is likely, if the change is at all large, that certain economies and substitutions will be made that are not reflected in the fixed technical coefficients of the model.'[2]

16. I dealt with the fundamental form of accounts in *Four Essays*[3] and it may be remembered that apart from a balance sheet this involved three main accounts, one for income, two for the appropriation of income, and three for capital changes. The last will obviously call for special mention, so that for the rest changes in formal aggregates concern the income and appropriation accounts. The changes in the latter from one accounting period

[1] 'Statistical Trends and Historical Changes', by Simon Kuznets, *The Economic History Review*, Second Series, Vol. III, No. 3 (Cambridge University Press, 1951), p. 277.

[2] International Association for Research in Income and Wealth, Third Conference, Castelgandolfo, September, 1953.

[3] *Four Essays in Accounting Theory* (Oxford University Press, 1953).

to another very largely depend upon the policy of the central government in regard to direct taxation, and the policy of those who direct an enterprise in regard to income distribution and saving. The effects of these policies operate after the determination of periodic income so that such changes as there arise are consciously determined. Accordingly, they are not so important from the standpoint of interpretation as those which vary periodic income measures.

17. An account which is meant to explain the application of saving must inevitably record capital changes, and in fact this account, as we have seen, has been rightly looked upon as the link between flows and stocks, or if you like, a semi-flow account reconciled with stock changes. Nevertheless, it is also a pure change account for differences in capital aggregates, and there is also another sense in which it can be regarded as a kind of 'jump' account for the notation of sudden and unforeseen changes in value. Besides showing sources of finance, it is also the home of capital gains and losses, and a place to pick up bygone errors and mistakes.

18. I think it is the study and development of the capital change account which has brought us to the recognition of a balance sheet as something more than the connecting link between successive income accounts. In fact, as it seems to me, a theory of asset preferences can only be worked out and understood with the aid of a capital change, and related income change, account. Regularities in asset preferences will involve relative changes of more or less variability. In a wider context, Goldsmith has suggested the 'analysis of structure of assets and liabilities of groups of ultimates and intermediary economic units with the purpose of ascertaining relations between balance sheet structure and economic behaviour, e.g. the influence of balance sheet structure on the saving function.'[1] There are even some economists, the leading protagonist would seem to be Boulding, who would regard the balance sheet as the central analytical concept of the theory of the firm, because they seek to explain the behaviour of economic organisms in terms of preferred asset ratios.

[1] *The National Balance Sheet of the United States of America 1900–1949*, by Raymond W. Goldsmith. International Association for Research in Income and Wealth—Third Conference, Castelgandolfo, September, 1953.

19. The essential task of accounting dynamics is the isolation and magnification of changes in accounting aggregates in order that we may study the changing economic pattern of an accounting entity. Such changes may be quite simply related or they may have relationships of a much more complicated order. Stone has a passage on 'Static and Dynamic Models' in which he says that:

The relationships in a static model connect variables belonging to the same time period whereas in a dynamic model this is not always the case and one or more of the relationships connect variables relating to different time periods. Many economic variables are clearly influenced by preceding events and in a sense, therefore, dynamic models, containing differences or derivatives of various orders, are superior to static models in representing the economic process.[1]

Ideas of the same kind are bound to show themselves when we come to consider relationships based on change accounts. In fact, I have been groping my way towards this point of view since September, 1949, when I said in a lecture on *Social Accounting* delivered in the University of Melbourne:

It might be inferred . . . that the accounting approach to the portrayal of economic information has little to offer in the way of a contribution to dynamic theory. For my part I am not so sure. If we can manage to construct . . . accounts for sufficiently short periods of time in succession, it may be that an examination of the finite differences will yield something to this developing theory.[2]

You may also remember that in my inaugural lecture delivered in this hall, I said that:

It is plainly our first duty to bring order and meaning into all recorded transactions which have taken place under one roof over a given period of time. The resulting epitomizations are essential factual presentations

[1] *Model Building and the Social Accounts: A Survey*, by Richard Stone. International Association for Research in Income and Wealth, Third Conference, Castelgandolfo, September, 1953.

[2] *The Accounting Mission* (Melbourne University Press, 1951), p. 24.

which tell their story within the limits of a static interval of time. They cannot be denied on any showing of stewardship, and they bring to notice some indispensable restrictions on business behaviour, but they do *not* complacently reveal *causal* or necessarily dependent relationships between categories. It may be that eventually those engaged in expectation accounting will want to know something about these relationships if, in fact, they can be shown to exist. For example, it might well be that real asset formation is for some entities induced by the trend of past outputs, accumulated saving and the present borrowing potential, rather than by current output and current saving. Yet again, for some members of society current consumption may depend upon penultimate rather than current incomes. I therefore advance the suggestion that such mental models as use aggregate variables drawn from customary accounts, and which rely upon functional lags to secure their premises, might be cast in special accounting forms made independent of the usual formal time period.

20. In economics dynamic analysis is especially concerned with relationships between past and present events. Samuelson, following on the view of Ragnar Frisch has said that: 'A system is dynamical if its behaviour over time is determined by functional equations in which "variables at different points of time" are involved in an "essential" way.'[1] This is essentially a mathematical approach but what I want to suggest is that a less sophisticated understanding of these things may be acquired from the money facts expressed in difference accounts. Again, Baumol is concerned with an examination of 'the relationship between the past and the present in some simple situations and to see how, given the initial situation, things may be expected to develop.'[2] He makes some interesting comments which seem to me to bear upon our subject. For example: 'Today's output depends on investment over the past, say, fifty years; the future prices a seller expects for his commodity depend on the prices he has experienced over the years in the past during which he has been in business, and so on.'[3] And yet again, '. . . . current output depends partly on

[1] *Foundations of Economic Analysis*, by Paul A. Samuelson, (Harvard University Press, 1947) p. 314.

[2] *Economic Dynamics*, by W. J. Baumol (The Macmillan Co., New York, 1951), p. 146.

[3] *Ibid.*, p. 142.

how much has been invested in production (purchase) and maintenance of capital equipment at each moment over a period of time. As a result (output being of the nature of a functional) it is not possible to relate current output to any single magnitude representing investment and maintenance over the entire period.'[1] Surely this type of comment suggests the relevance of periodical difference accounts, derived from historical accounts themselves. Baumol himself thinks of economic dynamics in terms of period analysis and says that: 'We may define it crudely as the splitting of time into periods such that, apart from exogenous changes, the events of any period can be explained with reference to the events of previous periods.'[2] It does seem to me that this is of the very essence of the accounting exercise itself. Moreover, it directly underlines the *raison d'être* for change accounts as a practical means of 'highlighting' income and capital changes over time in order that we may look for some backward and forward relationships in a general pattern of change. Indeed, it may very well turn out that change accounts are the vital link between historical accounting and expectation accounting. Perhaps we shall become even more concerned with estimates or standards of change, a not improbable development in accounting theory, and in this context there are some observations by Lindahl which we might do well to ponder over. He writes in this wise:

Starting from the plans and the external conditions valid at the initial point of time, we have first to deduce the development that will be the result of these data for a certain period forward during which no relevant changes in the plans are assumed to occur. Next we have to investigate how far the development during this first period—involving as it must various surprises for the economic subjects—will force them to revise their plans of action for the future, the principles for such a revision being assumed to be included in the data of the problem. And since on this basis the development during the second period is determined in the same manner as before, fresh deductions must be made concerning the plans for the third period, and so on.[3]

[1] *Ibid.*, p. 142—Footnote 31.
[2] *Ibid.*, p. 124.
[3] *Studies in the Theory of Money and Capital*, by Eric Lindahl (George Allen & Unwin Ltd., London, 1939), pp. 38–9.

Thus, we cannot but recognize the impelling force of change on our future plans, and we should remember that it is these plans which find expression in our expectation accounts.

21. It seems to me that changes in accounting aggregates can be formally classified in three ways. First, the plain and straightforward differences between the actual figures of two accounting periods, sequential or otherwise. Second, the variances between predetermined standard and actual figures which have become so familiar in the methods of cost accounting. Third, the differences between expected changes and realized changes which we might possibly look upon as exemplifications of exogenous variables. I shall want to suggest that our main concern in accounting dynamics is with the first and third of these classifications, especially the third because it fastens attention upon involuntary changes, e.g. unpremeditated deviations from investment intentions.

22. I suppose we should all admit that accounts are more informative when they are accompanied by such real and quantitative data as the number of people employed in their several categories, plant utilization and so on, for as Stone has said the main difficulty is with purchases of factor services, but always the accounting problem is the expression of quantities side by side with the relevant monetary aggregates. If this is true of the aggregates themselves then it is also true for changes in aggregates. Thus, if we could solve the problems for aggregates in some simple manner, we should also solve it for changes in aggregates. I do not expect we shall necessarily find simple and adequate solutions, but I should like to re-emphasize one or two relatively well-known ideas which look adaptable to this subject.

In *Four Essays*,[1] I set out a simple form of operating account with the input allocations for labour and capital described in the following detail:

LABOUR—Wages and salaries and social insurance contributions.

i. Direct or operative	x		
ii. Ancillary	x		
	—	x	
iii. Selling and distribution		x	
iv. Administration and management		x	
		—	x

[1] *Four Essays in Accounting Theory* (Oxford University Press, 1953).

CAPITAL—			
i. Rents (imputed or actual)			
1. Factory	x		
2. Warehouse and salesroom	x		
3. Office	x		
	—	x	
ii. Depreciation of *real* assets measured in terms of end-period prices		x	
iii. Interest on *real* assets (excluding buildings) employed during the period of account, and measured in terms of end-period prices ...		x	
		—	x

You may remember that I did make the suggestion that an unsophisticated form of operating account which contained these inputs was equally applicable to a department or process and that it could be made the subject of a time series. The immediate problem, however, is to find quantitative indicators which will add significance to their monetary counterparts so that money changes can be read in association with quantity changes. I first thought of handling this by picking out of the labour input the direct or operative and ancillary items and expressing them in terms of man hours. I have always recognized that when it comes to factor services time looks to be the constituent quantity pointer, and I thought of breaking down the sub-totals I have indicated into reasonable categories of more or less uniform units. It did not seem to me that this would be impossibly complicated when the entity of account was limited to a department or process, although it was obvious that a good deal of approximation would have to be contemplated for a larger entity, or possibly some form of weighting to give a few simple time indicators. I also thought I might deal with the capital input by picking out the item for depreciation and then, by separating off the 'user cost', express this in terms of machine hours.

But, having arrived so far, there still remained items in the labour input for selling and distribution, although this might have been related to quantities sold, and for administration and management. In the capital input, rents and interest on real assets remained to worry us; possibly space occupied might have been related to rents, and interest on real assets (excluding buildings) employed might have been made to follow depreciation. Thinking along these lines, primarily in terms of the significance of changes, it occurred to me that probably the best single quantitative time indicator for variable factor inputs, by which to measure changes and assess their significance, was still the standard hour as devised for an operation or a process; more especially as an operation or process in fundamental theory is itself an entity of account, and the standard hour unit is sufficiently homogeneous to be aggregative. Such a quantitative indicator could be easily noted on any form of operating account for the purpose of measuring productive efficiency.

This seems to be the place to revive mention of the following explanation which appeared in the report of a sub-committee of the Incorporated Accountants' Research Committee on the measurement of productive efficiency.

> 1. For every operation or process there needs to be fixed a standard output per hour, e.g. so many physical units to be produced in an hour. The total units produced divided by the standard hourly output gives the number of standard hours produced.
> 2. For each operation there should be recorded:
> (*a*) the total hours available;
> (*b*) the total hours the machine or cost centre is actually working; and
> (*c*) the standard hours produced.
> 3. From these figures:
> $\frac{b \times 100}{a}$ is the figure of capacity usage,
> $\frac{c \times 100}{b}$ is the operating efficiency, and
> $\frac{c \times 100}{a}$ is a combination of the previous two factors, which may be described as 'over-all efficiency'.[1]

I should add that I am indebted to Mr. C. E. Sutton for his continual recollection of this standard hour concept, and it does not need great imagination to see the relevance of a comparison between expected changes measured in standard hours and realized changes in standard hours.

23. Accounting dynamics then is concerned with controlled and repeatable measurements of economic events, as they affect a

[1] 'The Measurement of Productive Efficiency', included in *Four Essays in Accounting Theory* (Oxford University Press, 1953) as an appendix.

particular entity, and their differences. Although for the most part accounts do pin us down to the facts, I think we should once again notice the general subconscious association in most people's minds of repetitive with expected, and in this context especially take note of a philosophical warning from Professor Moore when he says that:

It is certain that in different circumstances the same action may produce effects which are utterly different in all respects upon which the value of the effects depends. Hence we can never be entitled to more than a *generalization*—to a proposition of the form. 'This result *generally* follows this kind of action'; and even this generalization will only be true if the circumstances under which the action occurs are generally the same.[1]

And perhaps with more particular relevance Seltzer has said that

. . . changes in expected receipts, unexpected changes in interest rates, and changes in the disposition to face uncertainties comprise the primary sources of 'pure' capital gains and losses.[2]

All this suggests that it is the interpretation of differences which is important as when we compare expenditures on research to improve products and services, in order that we may look upon a positive difference as evidencing the willingness of a management to keep its enterprise adaptable to changing technology.

24. There can be little doubt that we are operating in one small section of a field of study which is engaged in a timeless search for a fuller understanding of economic change, but even the accounting stronghold seems open to limitless variability of one sort or another. For example, on an issue which most of us thought we were beginning to understand:

Fabricant has pointed out ('The Varied Impact of Inflation on the Calculation of Business Income', reprinted in *Five Monographs on Business Income*, July 1, 1950, pp. 155–9) that the impact of inflation may be greater on the business accounts of one industry than on those of another. The factors involved are: (1) variation, among industries,

[1] *Principia Ethica*, by George Edward Moore (Cambridge University Press, Fourth Impression, 1948), p. 22.

[2] *The Nature and Tax Treatment of Capital Gains and Losses*, by L. H. Seltzer (National Bureau of Economic Research, 1951), p. 62.

in the importance of physical assets; (2) variation in the rate of turnover of physical assets; (3) variation in the average age—or year of acquisition—of capital assets; (4) variation in the rate of rise in prices paid for physical assets; and (5) variation in the accounting procedures followed.[1]

But perhaps there is a lesson for us in the following statement in rather different context, and with rather different relevance, taken from a report emanating from the Statistical Office of the United Nations in August, 1952:

Comprehensiveness of statistical data and the elaboration of relationships expressing economic behaviour assume a greater importance the smaller the number of variables that are determined in advance by acts of public policy.[2]

Business behaviour and business policy are, of course, our immediate concern. Nevertheless, we can get out of this a background to the manner in which we should try to work out actual change accounts in order that we may look for and think about some special change relationships.

25. Before we pass on to stricter matters of account, there are one or two further reflections on the nature of change, that I wish to bring to your notice. In the last resort, no doubt, change is inevitable and in the long run unpredictable. Professor Jewkes would have it that it is the rôle of economic science:

First, from its understanding of the nature of the economic scene, to make clear the inevitability and unpredictability of change; second, to suggest mechanisms and methods of measurement by which changes will be recognized as quickly as possible when they have occurred; and third, and most important of all, to search for and even to recommend those institutions which will enable men and societies to adjust themselves as easily and painlessly as possible to the inescapable vicissitudes of economic life.[3]

[1] *Changing Concepts of Business Income.* Report of Study Group on Business Income (The Macmillan Co., New York, 1952), p. 77.

[2] Statistical Office of the United Nations, August, 1952. *A System of National Accounts and Supporting Tables.* Report prepared by a Committee of National Income Experts appointed by the Secretary-General, New York, p. 8.

[3] 'The Economist and Public Policy', by John Jewkes, *Lloyd's Bank Review*, April, 1953, pp. 27–8.

Surely the same comments, or if we do not wish to claim too much, at least the second on mechanisms and methods of measurement, might very well have been attributed to the rôle of accounting itself. As you will suspect, as an accountant, I have great sympathy with such comments very largely because they bring matters into the realm of practical affairs where most of us have to justify ourselves, and perhaps, therefore, it will not be judged amiss if at this initial stage in the discussion of our own subject, we take another look at what Professor Jewkes had to say. Thus:

First, the use of economics is to provide data and not decisions; it can inform but it cannot prescribe. The best parallel is that of a map. The most important function of the map is to inform the traveller where he is, to provide a frame of references. It can tell him where he will get to if he travels in one direction or another, but beyond that it is neutral as to whether he travels north, south, east or west. Every wise traveller carries a map but no sensible traveller asks the map where he should go. So, too, with economics; although it should never be forgotten that, just as men may sometimes prefer not to take the shortest route between two points on the map, so economic motives are not always, perhaps not usually, the most important promptings of the human spirit.[1]

If we read 'accounting' for 'economics' we have a pretty accurate description of what the more cautious among us would regard as the modern function of accounting. And again, with a very precise bearing on our own immediate subject, he says that:

The economic future is an area of vast uncertainties; technical progress has never been more rapid, the ways of best making a living have never been more fluid, the probing for new knowledge has never been so determined. Statesmen should remember, with Francis Bacon that, 'The subtlety of nature is greater many times over than the subtlety of senses and understanding and that if a man will begin with certainty he shall end in doubts; but if he will be content to begin with doubts he shall end in certainty.' Economic security in the sense of freedom from change is a will-o'-the-wisp. Much that will occur will come as a surprise. Much that will be done will inevitably be mistaken. The efficiency of an economic system seems likely to depend, not upon how few mistakes are made but how quickly they are recognized and with what dexterity they are repaired.[2]

[1] *Ibid.*, pp. 29–30. [2] *Ibid.*, p. 32.

26. In discussing the nature of change, I have wilfully traversed a number of contemporary opinions before coming down to the technical implications for our own job, but before ending this part of the matter on hand, I want to take you right off the beaten track to exemplify what I will call the ladder of accounting entities. You will know, as I do, that accounting has been slowly developing on the aggregative plane. We have moved from consolidated or group accounting to social or national accounting, and we are now thinking of international accounting. You will remember that earlier on I made a point about the changing quality of large accounting aggregates and you will also remember that for some time now I have put forward a theory which seeks to apply universal concepts of structure, form, and measurement to any and every economic activity which requires to be viewed by means of accounts. Again, when we are considering the significance of accounting changes I think we must have special regard to the size of the entity whose accounts we are contemplating. I recently read a passage in Professor Gardner's Rede Lecture for 1953 which seemed to me peculiarly relevant. Perhaps I should explain that Professor Gardner is the Regius Professor of Medicine in the University of Oxford. I quote that passage in the hope that it will suggest to you a similarity of ideas. Thus:

> Above the level of the individual man we have the family, the institutions of society, nations and international organizations. In the animal and vegetable worlds we have species, genera and families of animals. From bottom to top there seems no logical break in the series, though at each level, as writers on Holism have pointed out, new and unique qualities appear. . . . It is curious that similar patterns of structure or function recur at different levels of organization.[1]

27. We now arrive at a point where technical considerations become important because 'accounting dynamics', as we have chosen to call our subject, is nothing more than an attempt at a precise approach to the general interpretation of accounts. We are trying to analyse what is really happening behind those aggregate

[1] *The Proper Study of Mankind.* The Rede Lecture for 1953 by A. D. Gardner (Cambridge University Press, 1953), p. 11.

figures which appear in accounts, in order that we may bring about a wider use of the figures passing through the hands of accountants. In a constantly changing society we need mechanisms and methods which detect sharp and unpredictable changes very soon after they begin to show themselves. Change when it occurs demands recognition and adaptability. In a general kind of way we are aware of a number of sensitive indicators, some of which lie behind the accounts themselves. For example, changes in inventories, in orders, in inquiries, and in production levels are indicators in point. A change in orders from a few very large ones to a number of small ones is significant. It needs to be smartly noted because it is very liable to bring about a marked decline in aggregate sales. Forecasts of expected sales can be seriously affected by out-of-step price changes; weather considerations may affect one industry, entertainment another. There may be a hard core of inelastic demand with a very elastic demand above and beyond a well defined point. Nevertheless, we are principally concerned with accounting changes. We have seen that the scale of the entity is important. Large-scale organizations may place more reliance on long-term trends and the consistency or inconsistency of patterns revealed by moving averages, and moving periodical totals. But always, if net earnings are to be kept in step, variable costs must be adjusted as quickly as possible to involuntary and inescapable changes in receipts. Price rises may depend upon revenue experience, but there is a vital distinction to be drawn between large-scale organizations with regular and necessitous outputs, and small- to medium-scale enterprises which have their home in industries occasionally beset by widely variable outputs. No doubt such variability may be determined by external considerations, but this only indicates the importance which should be attached to input-output analysis for enterprises in *all* industries. The sources and relative magnitudes of demand can and should be read in association with experienced individual accounting variability.

28. So far financial accounting variability seems to have been measured in terms of aggregate relationships. For example, operating labour cost is sometimes expressed as a variable to be

kept within limits determined in relation to total cost. Capital investment, especially inventory investment, and sometimes capital requirements are expressed as percentages of annual net sales or cost of sales, and occasionally as proportionates of factory labour costs. Ratios of the following types are commonly used in research studies:

Total assets as a percentage of net sales.
Inventories as a percentage of net sales.
Debtors as a percentage of net sales.
Liquid assets as a percentage of net sales.
Net fixed assets as a percentage of net sales.
Total assets as a percentage of factory wages.
Net fixed assets as a percentage of factory wages.
Owner's investment as a percentage of total assets.
Manufacturing costs as a percentage of net sales.
Labour costs as a percentage of cost of goods sold.
Selling and distribution costs as a percentage of net sales.
Administration costs as a percentage of net sales.
Profit before taxation as a percentage of net sales.
Profit before taxation as a percentage of owner's investment.

In our present discussion, however, we shall try out the measurement of variability in another way, principally by looking at relationships in terms of changes. To do this, we must examine the make-up of the change accounts themselves.

29. In my previous research lecture I gave a form of capital change account appropriate to the needs of public companies, and for rather obvious utilitarian reasons I named it, 'Sources, Earmarkings and Utilization of Funds'. On now looking at my presentation I am inclined to think that it was a little obscure because I tried to treat it as one main account. I now take the view that this account would have more meaning if it were broken down into certain well-defined sectional accounts, of which I distinguish five or six. The first of these should be confined to saving and asset formation, and owes its origin to certain social accounting ideas, which I think might be revived here as an aid to our understanding of its main purport. It has been emphasized by Keynesian economists that saving by one entity does not necessarily carry

with it an intent to use that saving on asset formation, although we do know that when the accounts of all entities within a closed economy are consolidated, then the aggregate accounting measure of saving is identically equal to the aggregate accounting measure of net asset formation plus net lending abroad. If we turn to individual accounts we can see which entities have done the asset formating and which have done the saving, or as in the more common business enterprise cases, those which have done both, thereby giving us a view of the dispersion of the individual deviations between the two. If accounting were simple and saving could be easily defined the deviation would be the balance on the sectional account for saving and asset formation. We know that for companies there are difficulties about adjustments to past income measures, earmarked items for redemptions and reserves, deferred liabilities for taxation and the like, but nevertheless, the source of the principle is clear. We shall also discover that for the individual enterprise there are a number of other important implications. In the case of a company, therefore, I should set up a sectional account for saving and asset formation in the following manner:

CAPITAL CHANGE ACCOUNTS

(i) Saving and Asset Formation.

1. NET EXPENDITURE on:			1. REPORTED INCREASE in undistributed income ...	x	
i. Tangible fixed assets ...	x		2. EARMARKED INCOME (redemptions and reserves)	x	
ii. Intangible fixed assets	x			—	x
	—	x	3. PROVISION FOR DEPRECIATION		
2. INCREASE (or decrease*) in deferred expenditure ...		x	i. Cost allocation	x	
3. INCREASE (or decrease*) in total inventories		x	ii. Price change adjustment*	x	
		—		—	x
		x	4. INVENTORY price change adjustment*		x
4. BALANCE—Excess saving ...		x			—
					x
			5. BALANCE—Excess asset formation		x
		—			—
		x			x
		═			═
* Negative			* Increase positive, or decrease negative		

There can be little question that this is one of the most important sectional accounts of capital changes. A very cursory reflection will suggest to us the possibility of a relationship between the changes in operating incomes of successive accounting periods and the real asset investment of earlier periods, which might be more precisely denoted as the changes in the outputs per employee of successive accounting periods and the real asset investment of earlier periods per employee. Thus we have a first reference to an income change account to be considered later. All this plainly links up with Baumol's observation that: 'Current output depends partly on how much has been invested in production (purchase) and maintenance of capital equipment at each moment over a period of time.'[1] I think it would also be helpful for economic analysis if we could analyse fixed asset formation in this sectional account into that part which relates to mere expansion, and that part which relates to innovation, and thereby arrive at expressions of both in terms of functions of changes in net outputs. Rostow has observed that: 'Changes in income may affect the incentive to accept innovations', and thereafter he talks about: 'The relation between income changes and the yields to be derived from the allocation of resources in different directions.'[2]

Keirstead seems to think, and some of us may hope that he is wrong, that:

With taxation of profits at the present level, it is less attractive to make large ventures in major innovations. The uncertainty is too great, the promise of net profit too small. Far more attractive is the process of minor innovations in design, in gadgets, 'selling-points', in ways of selling, in advertising 'campaigns'. (Since advertising outlay is regarded as a normal operating cost, it can be deducted from net income for taxation purposes. Thus the tax system frequently favours this kind of outlay as compared with outlay in the form of re-investment of net profits for the expansion of plant or the introduction of mechanical innovations.) Technical progress continues; wars have stimulated some major innovations, but the most important of these are now under the initiative and direction of government. It is at least possible that

[1] *Op. cit.*

[2] *The Process of Economic Growth*, by W. W. Rostow (W. W. Norton & Co. Inc., New York, 1952), p. 31.

future progress in private industry will be less dramatic than in the past, that major innovations will have to be subsidized in some manner by public funds or underwritten by government, and that, in conformity with a ruling passion, private industry will become more concerned with security than with progress.[1]

Even if innovations are to be crowded out, at least such fixed asset expenditure as is devoted to them seems, from this reflection, to be more directly related to retained income than to net output. Such a relationship should be readily discoverable from our sectional capital change account for saving and asset formation.

30. There are a number of useful accounting relationships which owe their derivation to this sectional account for saving and asset formation. For example, the rate of gross fixed asset investment (i.e. fixed asset formation before deducting the depreciation provision) can be expressed as a function of net output, and of *operating* income plus the depreciation provision. And again, the rate of net fixed asset investment (i.e. fixed asset formation after deducting the depreciation provision) can be expressed as a function of gross fixed asset investment and of *operating income.* A time series based on this kind of ratio should give an indication of the rate of growth of the *real* fixed asset investment of an enterprise. Moreover, this could be set up for classified groups of fixed assets, if the expenditures on tangible fixed assets and on deferred outgoings were suitably analysed in the sectional account. Nevertheless, it should be said that there are critics who hold that a relationship between output and asset (capital) formation is not entirely satisfactory because of variations in the degree of capacity utilization. They suggest that asset (capital) formation should be related to the difference between the capital stock of real assets required for production and the actual amount available, the capacity principle as it has been called. They hold that this would give a more satisfactory explanation of levels of asset (capital) formation in a number of industries. It seems to me that a similar relationship might be developed for changes in financial claims (i.e. asset claims less liability claims, or working financial capital)

[1] *An Essay in the Theory of Profits and Income Distribution*, by B. S. Keirstead (Oxford: Basil Blackwell, 1953), pp. 50–1.

which find their place in a later sectional capital change account. For those of you who may be interested, I give the following quotation:

As may be seen from empirical investigations of the acceleration principle, of which those by Kuznets[1] and Chenery[2] may be mentioned, it seems doubtful whether this relationship between output and capital formation is likely to bc satisfactory in practice largely because of variations in the degree of capacity utilization. An alternative relationship, in which capital formation is related to the difference between the capital stock required for production and the actual amount available has been termed by Chenery the 'capacity principle' and found by him to provide a more satisfactory explanation of levels of capital formation in a number of industries than does the acceleration principle. The alternative relationship, however, requires knowledge of the level of the capital stock in each industry measured in units which are comparable with the flow of capital formation. The promising nature of the relationship, therefore, adds further importance to the study of total and sector balance sheets. . . . [3]

31. You may remember that in my previous lecture on *The Formal Principles of Public Company Accounting*, I brought into the credit of the capital change account an item for inventory price change adjustment, and I positioned it as an inset along with saving and provision for depreciation. You would, therefore, naturally expect to find it in the sectional account for saving and asset formation in paragraph 29, but an inventory price change adjustment should not be looked upon in quite the same way as a price change adjustment for depreciation. The inventory one is a measure of an unrealized windfall *profit or loss* in money terms, which is a little different from that part of an imputed entry for depreciation required to transform an historical cost allocation into

[1] 'The Relation between Capital Goods and Finished Products in the Business Cycle', by Simon Kuznets, in *Economic Essays in Honor of Wesley Clair Mitchell* (Columbia University Press, 1935), pp. 209–67 and reprinted in *Economic Change* (Norton, 1952), pp. 47–104.

[2] 'Overcapacity and the Acceleration Principle', by Hollis B. Chenery in *Econometrica*. Vol. 20, No. 1, January, 1952, pp. 1–28.

[3] 'Recent Developments in National Income and Social Accounting', by Milton Gilbert and Richard Stone. International Statistical Institute, Conference at Rome, September 6–12, 1953. Published in *Accounting Research*, January, 1954.

a *current cost* measure. Inventory profits and losses can be peculiarly significant. Indeed, Keirstead says that: 'It is incorrect either to regard these windfalls as unimportant or to discuss them as being accidents beyond the entrepreneur's power of control. They, too, may be the object of expectations and hence a governor of the dynamic system.'[1] Moreover, when we come to review the implications of the capital change account as a whole, we should not overlook the fact that an accumulation of price change adjustments picked up on a rising price scale may need to be appropriated for income distribution purposes on a falling price scale. Nevertheless, if the credit entry for inventory price change adjustment is related to the debit entry for increase or decrease in total inventories in the sectional account for saving and asset formation, we can arrive at a current *money* measure of *real* inventory formation.

[1] *Op. cit.*, p. 14.

4
ACCOUNTING DYNAMICS—II

A research lecture given at Incorporated Accountants Hall, London, on 16th November, 1954

> This new tinge to modern minds is a vehement and passionate interest in the relation of general principles to irreducible and stubborn facts. All the world over and at all times there have been practical men, absorbed in 'irreducible and stubborn facts': all the world over and at all times there have been men of philosophic temperament who have been absorbed in the weaving of general principles.[1]

1. Inventory formation is an important item in the sectional capital change account for saving and asset formation, more especially when it is brought into relationship with items in other sectional change accounts, yet to be described. For example, a dangerous situation can be created when a large investment in stocks is financed out of a future tax reserve, because on a downturn of events, this can seriously upset a desirable and preferred liquidity ratio. A stock of finished goods is sometimes expressed as a time relation of sales, for example three months, in which case it is usually thought to be a matter of some consequence that increases or decreases in stocks should be kept currently consistent with this assumed constant. I think there are serious reservations in respect of this view, but before going into them I think we should notice the usefulness of such an analysis as is contained in a recent publication of the American Institute of Accountants on long-form report practice.[2]

2. In that survey a comparative summary of the inventories for two consecutive accounting periods is given which distinguishes between the increases and decreases in identified raw materials, and purchased parts, and between increases and decreases in

[1] *Science and the Modern World*, by A. N. Whitehead (Cambridge University Press, 1953), p. 3.

[2] *An Analysis of 52 Long-Form Reports*, by the Research Department of the American Institute of Accountants—including Selected Excerpts and Reproductions of 5 Complete Reports (The American Institute of Accountants, 1953), p. 71.

manufacturing materials, and work in process on identified products. It also gives the increases and decreases in finished parts and finished goods for identified products. It is my first point that such a supporting analysis of the total inventory formation included in the sectional capital change account for saving and asset formation is plainly desirable provided that it does not involve too many raw material and product categories for the one enterprise. My second point is concerned with the relationship between changes in inventory formation and changes in gross and net outputs as well as changes in the variable or gross profit margin. It seems to me that the inventory formation analysis which we are now considering presupposes the preparation of separate operating accounts for major product categories and it also logically requires that particular raw material categories should be allocated to product categories. In this way, the inventory changes in respect of raw material, purchased parts, manufacturing materials, work-in-process, finished parts and finished goods appropriate to one major product would be related to the gross and net output changes, and to the change in the variable or gross profit margin, for that *same* major product. In other words the major product category would become a subsidiary entity of account for the study of these special change relationships.

3. This immediately implicates us in a consideration of the form of the product operating account, and the accounting definitions of gross and net outputs, and the variable or gross profit margin. You will remember that in *Four Essays* I set up the first part of a general form of operating account in the following way.

Variable Inputs			Output		
4. Labour—Wages and salaries and social insurance contributions			1. Sales of goods and services ...	x	
i. Direct or operative ...	x		2. Minus Purchases of goods and services (directly varying with output)	x	
ii. Ancillary	x			—	
iii. Selling and distribution	x			x	
	—	x	3. Changes in inventories ...	x	
5. Variable Margin		x		—	x
		—			—
		x			x
		=			=

To avoid misunderstanding it might be as well to give a few examples of those items which ordinarily come under purchases of goods and services directly varying with output. I suggest the following:

I. Goods:
   i. Raw materials.
   ii. Manufacturing materials.
   iii. Consumable tools.
   iv. Intermediate—for example, purchased parts.

II. Outside services:
   i. Carriage inwards.
   ii. Power.
   iii. Intermediate—for example, commission work.
   iv. Other direct expenses.

III. Goods and outside services purchased in connection with the sale and distribution of the product.

4. We now have to particularize and open up the foregoing form of account in order to provide ourselves with the variable part of a detailed product operating account which is designed to give us accounting definitions of gross and net outputs, as well as the variable or gross profit margin. In the present context, and for the time being, we shall also want it to record the changes as between one accounting period and another. These objects may be achieved in the following type of account.

PRODUCT OPERATING ACCOUNT

		Period 1	Period 2	Change		Period 1	Period 2	Change
4. GOODS purchased (originating and intermediate)					1. SALES of finished goods and finished parts	x	x	x
i. Raw materials ...	x				2. Increase (+) or decrease (−) in stocks of finished goods and finished parts...	x	x	x
ii. Manufacturing materials ...	x							
iii. Consumable tools	x							
iv. Purchased parts ...	x							
	—	x	x	x	3. GROSS OUTPUT: ...	x	x	x
Forward ...		x	x	x	Forward ...	x	x	x

PRODUCT OPERATING ACCOUNT—*continued*

		Period 1	Period 2	Change		Period 1	Period 2	Change
Brought forward ...		x	x	x	Brought forward ...	x	x	x
v. Increase (−) or decrease (+) in stocks	x							
vi. Increase (−) or decrease (+) in materials (originating and intermediate) content of work-in-process ...	x							
	—	x	x	x				
		x	x	x				
5. OUTSIDE services (originating and intermediate)								
i. Carriage inwards	x							
ii. Power	x							
iii. Commission work	x							
iv. Other direct expenses ...	x							
	—	x	x	x				
v. Increase (−) or decrease (+) in direct expense content of work-in-process		x	x	x				
		x	x	x				
6. GOODS and outside services purchased in connection with the sale and distribution of the product. (Similarly adjusted for any possible increase (−) or decrease (+) in stocks of goods if these are brought into account, e.g. catalogues) ...		x	x	x				
Forward ...		x	x	x	Forward ...	x	x	x

PRODUCT OPERATING ACCOUNT—*continued*

	Period 1	Period 2	Change		Period 1	Period 2	Change
Brought forward ...	x	x	x	Brought forward ...	x	x	x
7. TOTAL consumption of goods and services directly varying with output	x	x	x				
8. NET OUTPUT or value added	x	x	x				
	x	x	x		x	x	x
10. LABOUR—Wages and salaries and social insurance contributions				9. NET OUTPUT or value added	x	x	x
i. Direct or operative	x	x	x				
ii. Ancillary to (i) ...	x	x	x				
	x	x	x				
iii. Increase (−) or decrease (+) in the labour content of work-in-process	x	x	x				
	x	x	x				
iv. Selling and distribution (directly varying with output) ...	x	x	x				
	x	x	x				
11. VARIABLE MARGIN ...	x	x	x				
	x	x	x		x	x	x

5. This form gives direct links between particular operating changes and particular inventory formations, and it is equally valid for classes of products and for departments. Moreover, it relates changes in gross output, in its categories of sales and stocks, to changes in cost classifications, both general and particular. It is therefore possible to develop a series of *change* ratios relating gross output to various categories of direct labour and not merely to the direct labour input as a whole. The same can be done for goods purchased and outside services. Such particular categories can be

selected and scheduled in supporting statements as desired. Again, a very special significance can be given to the development of a series of *change* ratios relating various categories of direct labour to value added or net output; providing always that proper deductions can be made about qualitative management factors, and the burden of capital input to be met out of the variable margin is *not* ignored.

6. It will be noticed that stocks and work-in-process are broken down and appropriated to their respective operating categories. This assumes that a clear distinction can be made between finished and unfinished work, and that at least the general categories of direct cost are readily identifiable in work-in-process valuations. It is my view that the general pattern of accounting changes and the validity of accounting ratios are impaired, where operating activity is concerned, if these assumptions cannot be made real. Thus, the increase or decrease in stocks of finished goods and finished parts is adjusted against sales to give gross output. Finished parts or finished components for which there is a market are treated as part of output in the same way as completed goods ready for sale.

7. The increase or decrease in stocks of originating and intermediate goods is adjusted against purchases to give a consumption total, but it should be obvious that a mere adjustment for *stock* changes is inadequate by itself, and that a further correction must be made for the increase or decrease in the materials (originating and intermediate) content of work-in-progress. If this is not done the measurement of net output as an independent variable is weakened. We are all familiar with the conception of materials consumed in production, but in accounting literature we seldom meet the suggestion that work-in-process necessarily contains a materials element which should also enter into any precise measurement of goods consumed. All too frequently a change in work-in-process valuations is treated as an adjustment either to the so-called prime cost of production or more likely, though with even less justification, the factory cost of production.

8. As we have seen, it is desirable that general categories of direct cost in work-in-process valuations should be readily identifiable if consumption variables on operating account are to be so

measured that they can be specifically related to outputs. It will be inferred from remarks in the previous paragraph that as a general rule I do not support the inclusion of overheads in work-in-process valuations despite, as it may seem, the views of the Inland Revenue to the contrary. I have dealt with this issue on two previous occasions. Thus, in *Social Accounts and the Business Enterprise Sector of the National Economy*,[1] I said,

it should be made plain that so far as concerns the inventory statement of unrecovered process costs the conventional accounting valuation is read as excluding standing costs covering the facilities of production where such costs are related to a continuing enterprise with a relatively large output of units of production. A modified statement of the operating account, in terms of variable and standing items, would make this clear by limiting inventories to the variable section. Thus:

MODIFIED OPERATING ACCOUNT

Opening inventories	x	Variable receivables	x
Variable payables	x	Closing inventories	x
Variable margin	x		
	x		x
Standing payables	x	Variable margin	x
Operating margin	x		
	x		x

It should be observed that standing payables are ordinarily related to standard outputs when it comes to a test of internal efficiency. So-called standard cost accounting procedure sets similar standards for variable payables and ordinarily seeks to measure inventory values on this basis. A statement of operating accounts in terms of variable and operating margins may be preferred by economists as constituting a first basis for an analysis which might emphasize marginal costs and revenues if applied to a series of short-term accounts.

Again, in *The Accounting Mission*[2] I said that:

In the plain economic view standing charges are regarded as necessarily

[1] Pp. 55–6 (University of Cambridge, Department of Applied Economics, Monograph 2—Cambridge University Press, 1949).

[2] Published for the Commonwealth Institute of Accountants by Melbourne University Press, 1951, pp. 31–2. (Great Britain: Cambridge University Press.)

incurred by an enterprise in providing its facilities of production and distribution. Once an entity is accommodated with those facilities it is bound to face the expenditure they entail, regardless of outputs, either produced or sold. We have to recognize that such standing charges are inescapable all the time that management chooses to engage those resources. This implies a retentive charge to activity account. Accordingly there is a case for asserting that standing charges should be dissociated from unrecovered costs pertinent to inventory valuation. The very simplicity of the argument invites a claim on our sympathy and there can be little doubt that it has much to commend it when we think of the dangerous ambiguities which can arise, in those cases where so called unrecovered standing charges are indiscriminately taken into inventory valuations. There are few of us who can deny that the mechanics of work in progress valuation are much simplified if we eliminate 'fixed expenses', for then it is possible to set up with a degree of directness such an activity account as gives to its component entries like characteristics and the resulting activity margin will appear as a plain conversion variable.

I do not think that for our present purposes I need add anything further to these explanations.

9. In the theory of product income presentation which so far we have been putting forward here, capital inputs have no part in work-in-process valuations because they are regarded as standing charges or fixed expenses, thereby falling outside the make-up of the variable part of the operating account. This is consistent with the treatment followed in *Four Essays* where, it may be remembered, the total capital input was regarded as a fixed expense commitment because its component parts comprised rents (imputed or actual), depreciation of real assets and, for a strictly theoretical purpose, interest on *real* assets (excluding buildings because covered by rents) employed during the period of account. As Cameron has remarked in the special context of the production function, 'the plant-entity is usually associated with equipment and services whose rate of input is invariant over the entire range of the plant's output—or at least the relevant portion of its range. The function is defined with reference to these fixed inputs—which in practice mainly refer to investment goods and

administrative services.'[1] It follows that negative differences brought about by a comparison of the actual amount of such fixed charges with the desirable levels determined by actual outputs, can be made to measure the ineffective surplus capacity effects of long-term errors in capital or asset formation.

10. And so we are left with the labour and direct expense contents of work-in-process valuations. The increase (minus) or decrease (plus) in the direct expense content of work-in-process is adjusted against the debit for outside services (originating and intermediate) in order to set up a functional relationship between services consumed and gross output. It is seldom the practice to bring into account stocks of goods specifically associated with expenditure on the sale and distribution of the product, unless such stocks are substantial, and the change from one accounting period to another is of sufficient magnitude to bring it within the category of deferred expenditure benefiting a later period. It could be that a major increase in a stock of new catalogues should come into account, in this fashion, for the purpose of a strict consumption measurement. Thus, in the first part of the product operating account we arrive at measures for the consumption of goods and services directly varying with gross output, and it seems that there is much to be said for a study, on the horizontal plane at least, of the effect of changes in the consumption of particular goods and services, and may be especially services, on the changes in gross output.

11. As a general observation to recapitulate our course, it should be noted that we are so far limiting our prospects to the *real* parts of difference accounts. The financial parts will concern us later in this study. As we have seen, the first part of our product operating account is essentially connected with the measurement of changes in the make-up of net output. In our attempt to understand this part of the account we shall assume that the material control procedures of cost accounting practice have taken care of the technical job of preventing waste and ineffective usage. Ordinarily, we might expect to find that any change from one accounting period

[1] *The Determination of Production*, by Burgess Cameron (Cambridge University Press, 1954), p. 20.

to another in the consumption of originating and intermediate goods was directly proportional to a change in gross output. In other words this relationship should be constant unless a technological improvement either in the method or instrument of production has brought about an economy in materials usage. A fall in the ratio of materials consumption to gross output might be directly relatable to a positive change in a particular part of the asset (capital) formation of a preceding or earlier period. An increase in the ratio of materials consumption to gross output is a matter for investigation if it cannot be ascribed to price. The consumption of outside services, however, may take on some of the characteristics of a factor supply. Thus, a positive change in some one service may give either an increasing or decreasing return. And so it becomes clear that the essential point *is* to study the related effect of changes on both sides of the account, and to judge whether a change in output has compensated for related changes in input. The more constant is the ratio of changes in total goods and services consumed to changes in gross output, the more significant becomes the relation between *net output* and factor inputs to be dealt with in the second and third parts of the product operating account, for then changes in net output are pointers to the marginal products of varied factor inputs.

12. Changes in gross output, apart from their relationship to changes in goods and outside services consumed, possess significance on their own account. It will be remembered that the divisible categories of gross output are: (i) sales of finished goods and finished products; and (ii) the increase or decrease in stocks of finished goods and finished parts. Changes in sales should be consistent with planned scales of output. Only quite recently it has been said of pronounced short-period changes that 'such fluctuations in turnover lead to higher costs since a rational utilization of the firm's capacity is impossible'.[1] There seems little question that changes in stocks of finished goods and finished parts should be proportionately related in some kind of way to changes in sales of finished goods and finished parts. In other words there should

[1] *Ten Years of Interfirm Comparison in the Swiss Retail Coal Trade*, by Karl Bründler. Translation of an article in the *Journal of the Management Institute of Zürich Technical University*.

be a correlation between the rate of growth or decline in finished goods and the rate of growth or decline in sales. It is well known that a steady accumulation of unsold finished stocks suggests that the production of particular products is out of line with the equilibrium level of the national product.

13. I think we should all *expect* to find a relation between a change in goods and outside services purchased in connection with the sale and distribution of the product and a change in the sales of the product itself, although this relation may neither necessarily nor immediately appear between the changes of the same time period. It may very well hold between the changes of different time periods; indeed a change in the one may very likely be related to a latent change in the other. Experience should tell us this, but the great purpose of this *expected* relation is to put us on inquiry if no such actual relationship shows itself.

14. It will be noticed that in our product operating account we have dealt with labour as a factor input, complete in itself, to be set against net output for the derivation of a variable margin. As a consequence, wages, salaries and social insurance contributions expended on the sale and distribution of the product are brought under the general heading of labour, although separately itemized in a sub-category at 10 (iv). We should expect the behaviour of this item to follow the same pattern as goods and services purchased in connection with the sale and distribution of the product, and the same considerations should apply. Accordingly, we should look for a relation between a change in wages, salaries and social insurance contributions expended on the sale and distribution of the product and a change in the sales of the product itself, although here again this relation may neither necessarily nor immediately appear between the recorded changes of the same time period.

15. It will be recognized that throughout this analysis of the operating account we are all the time seeking functional relationships between accounting aggregates, especially patterns of change relationships. Now we come to the labour input proper. The make-up of this input comprises wages, salaries and social insurance contributions expended in a direct or operative capacity, as well as that labour which may be described and classified as

ancillary to the operative category. We have already touched upon the significance of a relationship between direct labour and both the gross and net outputs, in paragraph 5 above, but the first point to be noted here is the adjustment to be made against the amounts expended on direct and ancillary labour for the increase or decrease in the same classified labour contents of work-in-process valuations. Again, the idea behind this particular adjustment is the achievement of a precise measurement of direct and ancillary labour consumed, because it is thought that this is the real variable which should be functionally related to both gross and net outputs, and at this stage in our discussion, especially the latter.

We have already noticed a passing similarity between the consumption of a factor of production like labour and the consumption of outside services. Thus, a positive change in direct and ancillary labour consumed may be accompanied by either a positive increasing or decreasing change in outputs, and the essential task is to judge whether such a change in outputs has compensated for the related change in input. As we noted in paragraph 11, the more constant is the ratio of changes in total goods and services consumed to changes in gross output, the more significant becomes the relation between net output and a factor input. Before we come to consider the more familiar notion of a production function, however, we should reflect on the possibility of a relation between the constituent content items of work-in-process valuations and stocks of purchased production materials on the one hand, and stocks of finished goods and finished parts on the other hand. More particularly, we should expect some kind of proportional relationship, which presumably experience will dictate, between changes in the materials content of work-in-process valuations and changes in the stock of originating and intermediate goods purchased, and probably we should expect both to alter in proportional relationship to changes in stocks of finished goods and finished parts. At the same time we should certainly expect the changes in the direct expense and labour contents of work-in-process to move in proportional relationship to the changes in stocks of finished goods and finished parts. If you prefer to look at it another way, it might very well be said that all changes in stocks and work-in-process should ordinarily move in proportional relationship to changes in outputs. Thus, if activity is expanding or contracting, or indeed stationary on an *equilibrium* basis (even keel, if so preferred), then these types of relationship would seem to be the natural expectations, and any deviations from experienced trends would take on unnatural appearances, and so require immediate explanations. In this way, deviations from normal expectations of all kinds of accounting relationships can be looked upon as measures to validate past management judgements as well as aids to management judgements in the future. It will be noticed that nothing has been said about the mathematical nature of these various kinds of proportional relationships because this is a matter for individual inquiry, individual experience and statistical study.

16. Schumpeter in describing what he calls the circular flow of economic life has said that 'one must treat combinations of means of production (the production-functions) as data, like natural possibilities, and admit only small variations at the margins, such as every individual can accomplish by adapting himself to changes in his economic environment, without materially deviating from familiar lines'.[1] Although we are probably misusing the purport of this quotation it can certainly be said that in the short period it is the work of accounting dynamics in private accounting[2] to bring to the immediate notice of entrepreneurs seemingly small variations at the margins of fundamentally conceived aggregates in accounts, so that they may indeed be sensitive to coming changes in their economic environment despite the veiling routine of familiar policies and practices.

17. We are now at a stage in our product operating account when we may think of the relation between direct and ancillary labour, as adjusted for the increase or decrease in the same classified labour content of work-in-process, and net output as revealing an important production function, more particularly if we are prepared to regard the capital input as relatively fixed in the short period, and entrepreneurial effort as similarly fixed. There are

[1] *The Theory of Economic Development*, by Joseph A. Schumpeter (Cambridge, Massachusetts, Harvard University Press, 1951), p. 80.

[2] This term is used in contradistinction to social accounting.

difficulties about both assumptions which we have introduced into this statement, because as we know any change in the capital input when it occurs, which is accounted for by a betterment in operating asset usage or technological improvement, will change this function. Moreover, as most of us are aware, the quality of entrepreneurial effort can be a decided variable despite the fixed expense carry in a later part of the operating account. Nevertheless, if we temporarily set aside these objections and ignore them as cutting across the short period, we can see how the marginal product of direct and ancillary labour varies as its input changes, and this is a valuable pointer to a state and scale of activity generating increasing, constant, or decreasing returns.

There are well-known measurement difficulties inherent in the formal concept of net output or value added when we are trying to set up a sectional operating account for either a plant-entity or a process whose concern is only with the part progress of a product in course of manufacture, even though we do assume the utilization of proper cost accounting techniques to prevent any wastage of either materials or labour. Some of these difficulties were hinted at in the preliminary report of a sub-committee of the Incorporated Accountants' Research Committee on 'The Measurement of Productive Efficiency'. Nevertheless, this representation of a production function can still be preserved for a plant-entity or part process by relating the direct and ancillary labour variable in money or man hour terms to the technical physical output of the plant-entity or process, and where necessary this can be expressed in the homogeneous unit of the standard hour. It will be remembered that in my first lecture on this subject I said that 'probably the best single quantitative time indicator for variable factor inputs, by which to measure changes and assess their significance, was still the standard hour as devised for an operation or a process; more especially as an operation or process in fundamental theory is itself an entity of account, and the standard hour unit is sufficiently homogeneous to be aggregative'.

18. It will be noticed that we have so far come upon a number of functions as revealed by the aggregates in the variable part of a product operating account, designed on lines consistent

with economic terminology, and we have especially looked for relationships between the changes in those aggregates. So far such functions as we have looked for have been self-contained within the pattern of the account itself, although not always discernible within the same time period. Goods consumed, both originating and intermediate, have been regarded as a function of gross output. Outside services consumed have been similarly regarded as a function of gross output, nearly akin to a factor supply function. It followed from both these functions that the aggregate for goods and outside services purchased and consumed in connection with the sale and distribution of the product should be regarded as a function of gross output. Direct and ancillary labour consumed has been primarily referred to as a function of net output, although wages and salaries and social insurance contributions expended on the activities of selling and distribution have been treated as a function of gross output. In all these cases we have emphasized the importance of comparing changes in inputs, either separately or in total, with related changes in outputs, or, if you so prefer, we have stressed that marginal approach which compares and contrasts marginal outgoings with marginal incomings. Thus, the marginal productivity of a change in inputs is the rate at which the output changes, a fundamental relation for all concerned. Output, however, has also to be considered and judged by a number of relationships which cannot be read off an accounting pattern in the shape of a product operating account. Current economic literature, especially that concerned with econometrics, makes use of a consumer-demand function to epitomize consumer behaviour. In a recent book, Cameron succinctly states the matter thus:

'Quantity demanded is a function of { income; own price; prices of other consumer goods.'[1]

He says that 'this is all the theoretical equipment needed to proceed to practical analysis where the prime problem is the

[1] *The Determination of Production*, by Burgess Cameron (Cambridge University Press, 1954), p. 32.

statistical one of actually specifying the form of and the numbers in the consumption function. However, it is possible to some extent to "go behind" this behaviour function and in particular to show how it expresses the actions taken by the individual as a result of economizing choice.'[1] Later he refers to a 'budget constraint' which, he says, 'stresses that you cannot spend more than your income' and he adds the significant comment that 'the budget constraint determines the scale of aggregate consumption expenditure'. It will be plain that all of this has to do with gross output, which is a resultant figure in our product operating account. Nevertheless, the consumer demand function as so far brought into use by econometricians is very largely concerned with national and industrial aggregates. This takes us back to the comments in paragraph 15 of my first lecture where I said that 'the object of management accounting should be the study of those economic changes which affect the firm. Such changes do *not* necessarily follow the same trends as those with which econometricians have been mainly concerned in their macrocosms. Thus, although it may be possible to give a likely estimate of the general aggregate demand for the products of a particular industry, nevertheless, there can still be substantial variability between firms.' I went on to say that because of the off-setting of errors of detail, there are better prediction possibilities when we are dealing with large aggregates, and once again I want to affirm my conviction that involuntary changes which are liable to affect *individual firms* should be detected immediately they arise, and in my view one of the best means of getting on to this is by way of a careful study of the *changes* in product outputs revealed in a short-period operating account.

[1] *Ibid.*, p. 32.

5

ACCOUNTING DYNAMICS—III

A research lecture given at Incorporated Accountants Hall, London, on 25th May, 1955

> Change is never complete, and change never ceases. Nothing is ever quite finished with; it may always begin over again. . . . And nothing is quite new; it was always somehow anticipated or prepared for. . . . We cannot hold together huge masses of particulars without putting into them some kind of structure. . . . Thus we are driven back upon periods. All divisions will falsify our material to some extent; the best one can hope is to choose those which will falsify it least. But because we must divide, to reduce the emphasis on any one traditional division must, in the long run, mean an increase of emphasis on some other division.[1]

1. In this series of lectures on the study of accounting we are trying to replace a juristic attitude with a scientific point of view. We began this process in *Four Essays*, where we dealt with the application of universal concepts of structure, form and measurement to any and every economic activity which required to be viewed by means of accounts. Our present concern is with a fourth concept which we call behaviour, for as it seems to us all accounting interpretations must depend upon discernible relationships in behaviouristic patterns of economic activity.

2. We justify this approach to the study of accounting on the grounds that the long-term future of any profession is influenced by its present encouragement of new points of view. This is one of the main purposes of the Stamp-Martin Chair. Professional institutions by the very nature of their constitutions are concerned to preserve well-tried and proven systems, but it must also be recognized that development depends upon the discovery and investigation of new ideas and new methods. If any further apology should seem to be called for, we would remind you that in the history of the professions it has often transpired that new ideas, even when they seem to lie at some distance from main

[1] *De Descriptione Temporum*, by Professor C. S. Lewis (Cambridge University Press, 1955), pp. 3–4.

interests, eventually become matters of vital concern with great utilitarian significance. In this and the next lecture, therefore, we shall continue to investigate and emphasize those methods of interpretation which are based on a firm's account of economic change.

3. You will remember that in our previous lecture we began the design of a product operating account in which the aggregate categories were decided on a conceptual basis in order that we might discover *standard* relationships whose variations over time would have some real meaning. We were looking for significant correlations within a logical framework. Correlations between empirically formed aggregate figures, whether part of an account or not, are bound to have their pitfalls unless the aggregates themselves are representative measurements of concepts which have a natural bearing on one another. To put it another way, a genuine correlation between aggregate figures is dependent upon the existence of a real underlying relationship between the concepts which those aggregates symbolize. As I said once before, 'unless there is some philosophical concord between variables there can be no more certain predictable relationships than are established by purely number relationships'. All this implies design, and as one writer has recently pointed out, 'a sort of "nonsense correlation" . . . merely indicates that methods of statistical inference are not independent of other forms of logic. The building of a realistic statistical framework on which data can be hung always calls for insight and intelligence.'[1]

4. Although our immediate concern is with the operating behaviour of firms, the development of standard relationships could have a much wider application, especially in those cases where profit is not the primary motive of economic activity. Moreover in national or social accounting we can think of the division of an economy into a number of sectors classified according to the constitutional and industrial differences affecting their behaviour, and with the aid of a formal pattern of accounts we could then watch the differences in their standard relationships.

[1] 'The Productivity Index in Active Service', by Stafford Beer. *Applied Statistics*, March, 1955, p. 4.

For example, a comparison of standard relationships and their rates of change (by means of change accounts) as between one particular sector of private enterprise and its counterpart industrial behaviour sector in Government or public enterprise would be instructive.

5. When dealing with firms and their product operating accounts we have been concerned to show how change relationships can emphasize marginal efficiencies. We have consistently posed the question—are these relationships improving or falling back on those already established as standard? In this context standard has reference both to the type of relationship and to its experienced measure, and at the level of general policy making there is a case for thinking that it is such relationships which should influence decisions. Thus, accounts designed on a simple formal basis to reveal logically dependent aggregates, and their changes from one accounting period to another, may tell a better and more easily assimilated story than some other designs based on the estimates of cost controls.

6. The change accounts with which we have been intimately taken up in this study give us short-term accounting information about incremental costs and revenues and enable us to observe the actual behaviour of costs with actual changes in outputs. For example, the change part of a product operating account will show us, as a result, the incremental costs of expanding the output of a specific product by a specific amount, and when we examine this against a background derived from the other product operations of a firm, we can take into account the level of outputs of other products which are being made and dealt in at the same time. This can be expressed another way by saying that the incremental cost of product *A* is a function of the production not only of *A*, but also of *B*, *C*, and *D*. As a consequence, therefore, we shall have to consider at a later point in our discussion the change relationships of a group of product operating accounts representing the total activities of the firm.

7. Any theory of formal or logically dependent relationships, such as we are seeking to set up in the accounting pattern we are now putting forward, depends in the last resort upon a concept of

normality when we try to impose measurement standards, and for this reason there is evidence for thinking that some of our standard relationships may turn out to be log normal, more particularly when they concern correlations between balance sheet and operating account aggregates. In this context we might also notice the suggestion that 'under certain assumptions the rational entrepreneur should attempt to vary his inventory levels (both purchase quantities and safety allowances) with the square root of sales rather than with sales'.[1] We should probably prefer to express this by saying that under normal conditions for certain specified trades past experience suggests that the rational entrepreneur should endeavour to control his inventory level proportionally with the square root of gross output. In fact, this will depend on his own estimate of gross output, and in this connection we should notice that such a relationship between a balance sheet aggregate and an operating account aggregate does not hold at the margin. Thus, *changes* in inventory levels will *not* vary with the square root of *changes* in gross output.

8. There has also been another very interesting suggestion, on the same lines, which Whitin tells us that W. J. Baumol plans to apply to monetary theory. 'The implication is that the quantity of money held for transaction purposes should be varied with the square root of total transactions.'[2] Presumably, for the firm, total transactions could be taken to mean the total receipts and payments of an accounting period. All this opens up a new line of approach to the study of standard relationships, especially when we are thinking about liquidity preferences or the adequacy of working capitals, but we should not forget that one of the mischiefs with accounting results is that we so often find an intricate intermingling of the normal and abnormal in the factual data on which they are based, and when we attempt to establish standard behaviour relationships for the firm of the type which is under discussion in this series of lectures, we may well find in practice that one of our problems turns out to be the isolation of necessitous but nevertheless abnormal items covered up in standard aggregate

[1] *The Theory of Inventory Management*, by Thomas M. Whitin (Princeton University Press, 1953; London: Oxford University Press, 1953), p. 95.

[2] *Ibid.*, footnote, p. 95.

categories. Yet, on a wider scale of reference, Whitin seems to rely upon the facts as they stand when he tells us that

. . . it is interesting to compare the relationships Keynes found between fluctuations in business activity and fluctuations in working capital with those that would exist if working capital varied with the square root of business activity. Keynes contended that the peak of business activity is '25 per cent above normal in the most severe cases and 13 per cent above in a credit cycle of average severity, with the trough correspondingly below', with working capital varying between '15 per cent from peak to trough in severe cases and 10 per cent in the more usual type of case'. If working capital varied with the square root of business activity, at the peak working capital would be 12 per cent above normal in the severe cases and 6 per cent above normal in the usual cases, while at the trough working capital would be 14 per cent below normal in the severe cases and 7 per cent below normal in the usual cases. The hypothesis that working capital varies with the square root of business activity is in closer agreement with the facts than the hypothesis that working capital fluctuates proportionately with business activity.[1]

9. In the context of the firm working capital and business activity would need to be specially defined. Most accountants are inclined to regard working capital as the difference between current assets and current liabilities, although up to now I have preferred to restrict the definition of this term to net financial claims plus speculative or abnormal inventories, and to think of business activity in terms of outputs. It should be mentioned that Keynes worked in constant prices, but for the purposes of our present inquiry what is interesting is his view of working capital, because it is different from and more partial than that of most accountants. Keynes says:

I define working capital as being the aggregate of goods (and the *cost* of working capital as the *cost* of the aggregate of goods) in course of production, manufacture, transport and retailing, including such minimum stocks, whether of raw materials or of finished products, as are required to avoid risks of interruption of process or to tide over seasonal

[1] *Op. cit.*, pp. 113–14 (The Keynesian references are to *A Treatise on Money*, Vol. II, Book VI, p. 111).

irregularities (e.g. intervals between harvests or fluctuations of individual harvests about the mean). It does *not* include surplus stocks, which constitute liquid capital. But it includes without distinction goods in process, such as foods and textiles, which will emerge as liquid income, the consumption of which will be spread over a short time, and goods in process, such as houses and railways, which will emerge as fixed capital, the consumption of which must be spread over a period, and are not immediately available.[1]

It is worth while spending a little time on this Keynesian idea of working capital, and because I think the emphasis on work in progress is instructive and may have some bearing on balance sheet classifications and valuations of assets, I add what Keynes regarded as the dependents of working capital.

The amount of working capital, thus defined, depends upon: (1) The rate of in-put (i.e. the rate at which the product has been started into the machine or process) over a period of past time equal in length to the duration of the process. (2) The intensity with which the factors of production are being and have been employed on a unit of the product at each stage of the process. (3) The duration of the process upon which the factors of production are employed. (4) The rate per unit of time of the cost of production, i.e. the rate of earnings of the factors of production per unit of efficient work applied to the product; which we may call, for short, the rate of wages. (5) The value of the stocks which must be carried to tide over the irregularities of the seasons.[2]

10. I ask you just to notice the use of the word 'efficient' in relation to the rate of earnings of the factors of production per unit of work applied to the product, but the really important narrow issue I do want to bring out from the references I have cited is the clear indication that a normal effective inventory carry is itself a balance sheet variable, not only in total but in all probability differently as between its constituent parts of materials, work in progress and finished goods, even though the total does not include the surplus stocks which Keynes would regard as constituting liquid capital. This again opens up the wider issue of a balance sheet qualification of all assets (and liabilities) which do not come

[1] *A Treatise on Money*, Vol. II, Book VI, p. 116. [2] *Ibid.*, pp. 116–17.

under a strictly fixed qualification, according to their degree and rate of variability with some operating aggregate; and thereby it incidentally vindicates the use of the term 'fixed' as applied to those assets which show no such proportional variability. Nevertheless, it does make suspect any suggestion of precision about the use of the generic qualifying term 'current'. This seems to me to clear up some uncertainty about the usual balance sheet arrangement of assets.[1] As I see it, this arrangement can now be thought of as a normal statistical division between fixed and variable, with the former justifying itself in accordance with scales of outputs achieved so as to negative *voluntary*[2] surplus capacities, and the latter in accordance with dependent operating aggregates, the balance sheet terms of which relationships may shade down from quasi-fixed to liquid. Moreover, I think we can see, from all that has been discussed, that behaviour relationships which are linked to balance sheet aggregates are likely to have different characteristics from those which derive from bilateral change accounts.

11. This brings me to a revision of my own ideas on the balance sheet statement of inventories. In *Four Essays*[3] I took the view that 'in so far as the major portion of the inventory of an enterprise *does* constitute a fixed asset necessary to the *continuation* of effective operations . . . it should be classified as such in the balance sheet' and later I added the comment that 'the essence of the inventory problem resides in the fundamental distinction between fixed and speculative holdings'. Accordingly, at that time, I put *standard* inventories with the fixed assets and *speculative* inventories with the short-term asset claims. Although the *speculative* part can be thought of in Keynes's terminology as surplus stocks constituting liquid capital, it now seems to me that there is more than a doubt about the inclusion of the *standard* part in fixed assets when we come to regard the term 'fixed' in the

[1] In *Four Essays in Accounting Theory* I said that 'I have never quite understood what was meant by the qualification "fixed" as applied to assets, moreover I have never quite touched bottom on the fundamental distinction between fixed and current assets' (Oxford University Press, 1953), p. 8.

[2] As distinct from *involuntary*.

[3] p. 38.

light of a statistical qualification. It is probable that there *is* always a constant real residuum in the inventory of an enterprise concerned with the effective continuation of its operations, but it would be difficult to define and measure, and having regard to the 'Whitin' type of inventory relation with output and the Keynesian working capital dependents, it now seems that we ought to regard standard inventories, and their constituent parts, as variables linked in some definable relationships with operating aggregates. It is plain that if we are to treat a standard inventory as 'fixed' in our new sense, then it must imply constant proportions between materials, work-in-progress and finished goods, and what is more important, but quite unlikely, constant outputs; thus the enterprise would need to be operating in conditions of constant returns.

12. We now begin to see the outline of a balance sheet classification of non-fixed assets which has regard to their effective rates of variability with operating and other aggregates. The standard effective inventory relation with gross output has been dealt with in some detail. We have received a hint of a possible effective relation between bank and cash balances and the total receipts and payment of an accounting period. Other relationships of the same order (expressible in a mathematical function but not necessarily direct) suggest themselves between debtors and sales, and creditors and purchases. If our operating expectations can be made reasonably reliable—and in the last resort this very largely depends upon the accuracy of our output estimates—we can derive from our knowledge of these several kinds of relationships standard balance sheet aggregates for non-fixed or variable assets (and liabilities). If we can then make a calculation for known or expected involuntary influences we are in a position to assess the significance of any variances from calculated standards that may be thrown up in the periodical accounts. For example, if inventories, debtors, or bank and cash balances are too high having regard to the standards calculated from the type of relationships we have discussed, it could suggest an ineffective use of the resources locked up in those asset categories. In short, we can regard all the various kinds of relationships between accounting aggregates, discussed and to be discussed in this series of lectures, as giving a complete, balanced,

and constrained view of the expected transactions of an entity in a state of effectiveness, always provided that such an entity can reasonably estimate its oncoming outputs and know something of their implications with the aid of a good background statistical intelligence.[1] Again, the capital and income change accounts, with the bilateral direct marginal relationships which they reveal, can be used for detecting the results of expansionist or contractionist policies, thereby facilitating the assessment of the short-term equilibrium position of the firm.

13. In a modified way we have come to the position that in the theory of the firm, estimates of voluntary or involuntary product demands are the main decision-making promoters, and in conditions of normal markets for both factors of production and their products, consumer behaviour can be thought of as the ultimate regulator of all accounting forms and relationships. This is why I tend to regard estimates of gross output as partially causative when it comes to the preparation of a formally derived accounting structure for a productive enterprise. Nevertheless, we continually need to ask ourselves whether these formal patterns and their consequential relationships can be held taut in the required order of a perfect use of resources. In practice, we know that such perfection is most difficult to attain, yet with a good show of reason we can argue that our formal structure—which is really nothing more than an aggregate background and a simple medium of comparability—displays a seemingly ideal view of proposed transactions given the assumptions on which it is based, and that such an accounting picture will keep us on guard against skew limpidities. Demand estimates can be subject to indefinable considerations of goodwill, and consumer behaviour looked at on a broad scale is governed by a hard core of necessary inelasticity shading down to the sensitive elasticity of imposed but changing tastes.

14. I now return to the more technical side of my subject and in so doing resume the discussion on the formal design of the operating account. It will be remembered that I especially

[1] See 'The Use of National Statistics in Industry', by John Ryan and D. J. Liston (*District Bank Review*, March, 1955).

drew attention to the fact that work-in-progress valuations usually contain three direct cost elements: namely materials, direct expense and labour. I also made mention of the fact that some firms include operating overheads in their work-in-progress valuations, but I gave reasons why, as it seemed to me, this was wrong in principle. I pointed out that for the purpose of calculating net output it would be an advantage if the general categories of direct cost could be identified in work-in-progress valuations, although I recognized there might be practical difficulties. I explained that composite figures for the opening and closing work-in-progress valuations of an accounting period, even when these measures look consistent, can veil *changes* in material, labour and direct expense contents, not to mention operating overheads.

Thus, an item for the goods consumed in an accounting period was inaccurate if an increase or decrease in *stocks* was the *only* adjustment made against purchases to give a consumption total. A further correction should be made for the increase or decrease in the materials content of work-in-progress. Similarly an increase or decrease in the direct expense content of work-in-progress should be adjusted against outside purchases. But, what was more important for the measurement of net output, an increase or decrease in the labour content of work-in-progress should be dealt with as an adjustment to wages and salaries and national insurance contributions.

15. In my last lecture and in the design of the first part of the product operating account which I then put forward, I was very largely concerned with such unifying conceptual measures, and their make-up, as net output (or value added) and the variable margin. It has since occurred to me that there is a conceptual difference between an accounting view of net output and the strict economic view of the same term, which ought to be made clear. In so far as a firm is concerned with the measurement of net output as a concept of use for its own purposes it will normally follow an accounting line by restricting such a measure to the difference between gross output and the consumption of goods and services varying with that output. As I indicated in detail in my last lecture,

a firm will do this because it is interested in the following main relationships, their make-up variants, and their rates of change:

i. Goods and outside services consumed, and gross output.
ii. Operative and ancillary labour, and net output.
iii. The variable margin, and gross/net outputs.
iv. Operating overheads, and net output.

For the wider purposes of input-output analysis with which economists are concerned and on a strictly theoretical census view, *all* goods and services purchased from outside should enter into the figure of net output. As a consequence, I think it should be made clear that those goods and services purchased from outside which are *not* treated by a firm as varying with output, and which I propose to show in a separate category in the continuation of the product operating account, should also be regarded as a deduction from gross output, as well as actual rents paid in the capital input, in arriving at a figure for net output in the strict economic sense of that concept.

16. It is interesting to notice that the accounting concept of net output, although only recently brought to the fore in this series of lectures, is borne out in a useful book on farm management published for the Ministry of Agriculture and Fisheries.[1] In a section on intensity of farming we meet the observations that 'two useful measures of the volume of business are the value of gross output per farm and the value of net output per farm. These may be converted to measures of the intensity of land use by dividing them by the farm acreage.' The gross farm output is expressed in terms of 'the total value of all sales of agricultural produce adjusted for the differences between the opening and closing valuations of crops and livestock, less the value of any purchases of livestock and livestock products during the year. The gross output of the farm is then divided by the farm acreage.'

We are then told, and this is the interesting point, that the value of net output per acre 'is almost the same in use and purpose as gross output since it is derived by subtracting the value of pur-

[1] *The Farm as a Business. A Handbook of Standards and Statistics for use in Farm Management Advisory Work.* Published for the Ministry of Agriculture and Fisheries by Her Majesty's Stationery Office, 1954.

chases of foods and seeds from gross output and dividing by the farm acreage. Purchasing foods and seeds is virtually a process of *borrowing* additional land. Not all farmers depend on the buying of food and seed to the same extent and so by removing this variable element a better comparison can be made.'[1] I would especially ask you to notice the reference to the removal of the variable element for the purposes of a better comparison. You will also recognize that both labour and the purchases of outside goods and services *not* varying with output are excluded from this measure of net output. I think it might be well to mention that because I regard net output, in the strict accounting sense, as the critical measure, I prefer to restrict gross output in a manufacturing enterprise to sales of finished goods and parts adjusted for the increase or decrease in stocks of finished goods and finished parts. This restriction is plainly necessary when we are concerned to establish relationships between the consumption of goods and services varying with output and gross output itself including their rates of change.

17. In the interests of accuracy I think I should mention that in items 7 and 10 (iv) of the first part of the product operating account I used the expression '*directly* varying with output'. I think the word 'directly' should be dropped because a mathematical implication could be read into the type of relationship I was discussing, which was not necessarily intended. Moreover, as we have seen, there are degrees of variability. Accordingly, item 7 should read 'Total consumption of goods and services varying with output', and item 10 (iv) 'selling and distribution (varying with output)'.

18. The second part of the operating account, which we are now called upon to consider, is concerned with the purchases of goods and services related to operating facilities and not ordinarily varying with output in the short period. It will also have regard to wages, salaries, remuneration and social insurance contributions allocated to standing overheads, and to administration and management. The final input before the derivation of that all-important variable—operating income—will be the capital one

[1] *Ibid.*, p. 21.

composed of rents and depreciation of operating assets, both of which can be thought of as reasonably invariant in the short period, as was noticed in the previous lecture. The productivity of the facilities represented by standing charges or fixed expenses 'is closely related to the quantity of variable resources with which they are combined'. Accordingly, it is important to make the most effective use of those facilities and 'to secure a proper balance between fixed and variable costs'.[1] There are at least six standard relationships which seem to me to have some bearing on this point. I give them below.

i. Operating overheads, and the total consumption of goods and services varying with output.
ii. Operating overheads, and the variable labour input.
iii. Operating overheads, and the total variable inputs.
iv. Operating overheads, and net output.
v. Operating overheads, and the variable margin.
vi. Operating overheads, and gross output.

It is not difficult to see that other variants of numbers i to iii might be more specially relevant: for example, operating overheads, and direct expense (represented by outside services) plus direct and ancillary labour. Nevertheless, of those I have given I tend to regard number iv as being the most important because it expresses the relation between value added from operating activity and total short-term fixed costs. It should be possible from this relationship to make a judgement on whether or not the resources of an enterprise are employed at a level consistent with the fixed costs involved. It should perhaps be mentioned that both the gross and the net output relationships can be expressed in terms of a stated amount of operating overheads, for example, one hundred pounds.

19. In Appendix III of my monograph on *Social Accounts and the Business Enterprise Sector of the National Economy*[2] I gave a suggested form of primary accounting return which attempted a detailed classification of the items coming under the heading of

[1] *Op. cit.*, p. 22.
[2] University of Cambridge, Department of Applied Economics, Monograph 2 (Cambridge University Press, 1949).

purchased goods and services. This form was based on a fairly wide selection of balance sheets and profit and loss accounts, and some use has already been made of it when dealing with the make-up of goods and services varying with output, as shown in the first part of the operating account. When dealing with the primary return I indicated that certain of the classifications—for example, where some uncertainty might be expected, as in the case of repairs and maintenance of buildings—should *not* include any wages of the employees of the enterprise, as such payables would appear under the headings for wages. This is also the view taken in the present series, for as we have seen it is especially necessary to make this distinction if we are concerned with the strict economic concept of net output. Therefore, in the general utility design of the accounts so far put forward and to be put forward, services means *outside* services. As a consequence, in the second part of the operating account the wages of employees engaged on, or allocated to, an entity's own repair work will come under the heading of labour allocated to standing overheads. I now again make use of the primary accounting return to give the following items as representative of those likely to fall under the classification of purchased goods and services related to operating facilities and not immediately varying with output.

i. Banks (and other financial intermediaries)—commission charges for keeping accounts.
ii. Cleaning.
iii. Insurances.
iv. Lighting and heating (in so far as this item is not a variable dependent on output).
v. Machine rents.
vi. Minimum or standard royalties.
vii. Postages, telephones, telegrams, and such like items.
viii. Printing and stationery.
ix. Professional charges.
x. Rates.
xi. Repairs and maintenance of buildings.
xii. Repairs and maintenance of plant and machinery.

xiii. Servicing of transport equipment.
xiv. Trade subscriptions.
xv. Travelling and entertaining.
xvi. Water rates.

20. I now set up the second part of a general form of operating account in the following way:

				Period 1	Period 2	Change		Period 1	Period 2	Change
13. PURCHASES of goods and services related to operating facilities and *not* immediately varying with output:							12. VARIABLE MARGIN:	x	x	x
i. Banks (and other financial intermediaries)—commission charges for keeping accounts										
ii. Cleaning* ...		x								
iii. Insurances		x								
(*a*) Factory	x									
(*b*) Warehouses and salesrooms	x									
(*c*) Office and General	x	x								
	–									
iv. Lighting and heating (in so far as this item is not a variable dependent on output)										
(*a*) Factory	x									
(*b*) Warehouses and salesrooms	x									
(*c*) Office ...	x	x								
	–									
v. Machine rents		x								
vi. Minimum or		x								
standard royalties		x								
		–	–	–	–	–		–	–	–
Forward ...		x	–	–	–	–	Forward ...	x	x	x

				Period 1	Period 2	Change
Brought forward...		x	–	–	–	–
vii. Postages, telephones, telegrams and suchlike items ...		x				
viii. Printing and stationery ...		x				
ix. Professional charges ...		x				
x. Rates						
(*a*) Factory	x					
(*b*) Warehouses and salesrooms ...	x					
(*c*) Office ...	x	x				
xi. Repairs and maintenance of buildings*						
(*a*) Factory ...	x					
(*b*) Warehouses and salesrooms	x					
(*c*) Office ...	x	x				
xii. Repairs and maintenance of plant, machinery and equipment*						
(*a*) Factory ...	x					
(*b*) Warehouses and salesrooms	x					
(*c*) Office ...	x	x				
xiii. Servicing of transport equipment*						
(*a*) Factory ...	x					
(*b*) Warehouses and salesrooms ...	x					
(*c*) Office ...	x	x				
Forward ...		x	–	–	–	–

		Period 1	Period 2	Change
Brought forward	...	x	x	x
Forward	...	x	x	x

				Period 1	Period 2	Change
Brought forward ...		x	—	—	—	—
xiv. Trade subscriptions		x				
xv. Travelling and entertaining						
(*a*) Works ...	x					
(*b*) Sales and distribution	x					
(*c*) Administration and Management	x	x				
	—					
xvi. Water rates						
(*a*) Factory ...	x					
(*b*) Warehouses and salesrooms	x					
(*c*) Office ...	x	x	x	x	x	x
	—	—				
14. LABOUR—Wages, salaries, remuneration and social insurance contributions allocated to:						
i. Standing overheads						
(*a*) Repairs and maintenance of factory buildings ...	x					
(*b*) Repairs and maintenance of factory plant and machinery	x					
(*c*) Servicing of factory transport equipment	x	x				
	—					
(*d*) Repairs and maintenance of warehouse and salesroom buildings		x				
	—	—	—	—	—	—
Forward ...	x	x	x	x	x	x

	Period 1	Period 2	Change
Brought forward ...	x	x	x
	—	—	—
Forward ...	x	x	x

				Period 1	Period 2	Change
Brought forward ...	x	x	x	x	x	x
(*e*) Repairs and maintenance of warehouse and sales-room equipment ...	x					
(*f*) Servicing of transport equipment—sales and distribution ...	x	x				
	—					
(*g*) Repairs and maintenance of office buildings ...	x					
(*h*) Repairs and maintenance of office equipment	x					
(*i*) Servicing of office transport equipment ...	x	x	x			
	—	—				
ii. Administration and Management						
(*a*) Office staff	x					
(*b*) Administrative directors ...	x	x	x	x	x	x
	—	—				
15. CAPITAL:						
i. Rents (imputed or actual) ...						
(*a*) Factory ...	x					
(*b*) Warehouses and sales-rooms ...	x					
(*c*) Office ...	x	x				
	—	—	—	—	—	—
Forward ...	x	x	x	x	x	x

	Period 1	Period 2	Change
Brought forward ...	x	x	x
	—	—	—
Forward ...	x	x	x

				Period 1	Period 2	Change
Brought forward ...	x	x	x	x	x	x
ii. Depreciation of operating assets						
(*a*) Factory buildings ...	x					
(*b*) Factory plant and machinery	x					
(*c*) Factory transport equipment	x	x				
(*d*) Warehouse and sales-room buildings ...	x					
(*e*) Warehouse and sales-room equipment ...	x					
(*f*) Transport equipment—Sales and distribution	x	x				
(*g*) Office buildings ...	x					
(*h*) Office equipment (including furniture and fixtures) ...	x	x	x	x	x	x
Total operating overheads ...				x	x	x
16. OPERATING INCOME: ...				x	x	x
				x	x	x

	Period 1	Period 2	Change
Brought forward ...	x	x	x
	x	x	x

* These classifications should not include any wages of the employees of the enterprise, as such expenditure should appear under the heading of labour allocated to standing overheads.

Note: This account may be supported by detailed schedules of the changes in individual items which on investigation can be separately related to some other variable category in the accounts.

6

ACCOUNTING DYNAMICS—IV

A research lecture delivered at Incorporated Accountants Hall, London, on 8th December, 1955.

> 'Ideal precision and rigor—the great virtues of analysis as such—have the price of requiring "abstraction from" all but the few elements and relations within experience which can be very clearly grasped together in one unified analysis. Width of vision—adequacy of a conceptual scheme for dealing with the whole of its empirical subject matter—is also essential for any great scientific achievement, and is generally attainable only at the cost of something less than perfect clarity, precision, and logical rigor.'[1]

1. In the previous lecture we completed the form of what might be described as the real part of income measurement. That is to say we ended a general form of operating account at the point where we derived a measure of operating income. As we have said all the way through, this unified view of operating transactions and their aggregate changes, is primarily intended to serve the needs of policy directors. It has been designed to give them broad frequent indicators to mark the trend of events both through the immediate past and into the immediate future. It can be said therefore to institute inquiry from the top downwards in the management of a firm's affairs, in contrast to other forms of accounting technique based on variability which usually start from centres of control, thereby working from the bottom upwards. As a matter of practical interest, I mention in passing that I know of an organization which has experimented with the simple set-design put forward in this series of lectures. It found that a formal review of the standard and change relationships appropriate to the periods covered drew attention to management weaknesses which were hinted at in the detailed routine variability reports which came from its own cost office. As a consequence of this unexpected check the cost office reports received closer attention at top level, correcting remedies were better understood

[1] Schumpeter's History of Economic Analysis, by O. H. Taylor. *The Review of Economics and Statistics*, February, 1955 (Harvard University Press), p. 17.

and decisions were made more rapidly than had been the case before.

2. A number of operating standard and change relationships, based on the formal properties of the account itself, have been so far proposed. It is necessary to point out, as has been remarked before, that this is not all. There are also a number of other and underlying relationships which can sometimes affect short-period estimates of the conceptual aggregate categories in the operating account. I give you some interesting recent examples taken from current literature. In *Applied Statistics* for March 1955, Mr. A. W. Swan describes a method of graphing sales figures for executive use in an organization where there is forward buying and—this is the important point—he suggests a relationship between stock changes and forward buying by customers. The latter he arranges in the shape of a future buying index which he constructs in the following way. I quote his words:

> Regarding orders for the 'current' month as 100 per cent, find the corresponding percentage values for 'first month' and 'second month' ahead. Add these two to form a 'future' buying index. The reason for taking each relationship, first month to current and second month to current, into account is that the first and second month lines behave independently and their relative position is important.

Mr. Swan suggests some interesting deductions from a relationship between surplus (i.e. available) stocks and his future buying index as adapted to a particular illustration. Thus,

> during a slump the customer does not care how big the supplier's stock may be. As, however, signs of improvement begin to appear he does begin to wonder about his future supplies . . . As the improvement accelerates and surplus stocks continue to fall the buyer becomes increasingly anxious about his future supplies and increases his forward orders, with a rate which varies inversely as the square of the surplus stock.

Mr. Swan points out that it would be dangerous to draw too rigid conclusions from his one example, but it does appear that the control of surplus stock may be more closely linked with buying confidence than has been realized; in the particular case under examination it would seem advisable to hold the level of surplus stock somewhere to the left of the bottom of the curve, high enough to maintain confidence by the buyer and yet low enough to avoid locking up too much capital. This would correspond to a future buying index varying between 80 and 120.

This is plainly a very interesting suggestion.

3. In the N.A.C.A. Bulletin for June, 1955, Section 1, there is an original and invigorating article by Mr. C. B. Allen introducing model building to accounting data. Mr. Allen believes that the structure of accounting is itself an economic model showing in terms of money the operation of a business, and I should wish his article to receive all the prominence it can get in accounting circles because I have frequently sought to make this very point. In his article Mr. Allen works up a simple model based on the customary form of income statement. He suggests a series of simple equations which can be developed and manipulated to give relations capable of indicating to management those operating factors which should be attacked when results are unfavourable. 'Depending on the situation some factors will be more susceptible *to change* than others.'[1] As has often been pointed out a straightforward operating account is itself an equation of which the aggregate categories constitute the symbols. Mr. Allen introduces other symbols to express operating relationships on a unit basis. Later he brings in more symbols, two of which seem especially relevant to the formal properties of our operating design. As we are on the threshold of an important development in accounting theory comparable to econometrics in economics, I quote his later symbols as well as the closing comments in his article.

> R standing for the Ratio of shipment units to sales units (which allows for sales returns, and perhaps other things).
> C standing for the Change in inventory of finished units (all of which is a production scheduling problem of its own).
> G_u standing for the variable cost of finished goods in inventory . . .

[1] p. 1331 (Italics mine).

Then we will come up with another condensed model for variable cost:

$$v=(RU\pm C)\ v_u \pm CG_u$$

or, translated, variable cost is determined as follows: sales units are increased by a factor to allow for returns, into shipment units; these are then converted into production units by considering change in finished inventory; these units are then costed at the unit variable production cost rate; to this amount is added or deducted the number of units added to or withdrawn from inventory, at the variable cost inventory valuation. From here, you can go on and project changes in costs from changing the factors involved.

When you are finished with this family of equations, you can start a few new ones by making further models of each factor in the variable cost equation, and working with them. You will then have your 'foot in the door' on model building.[1]

As Professor Sir Ronald A. Fisher once remarked: 'Since Euclid's time there have been very long periods during which the right of unfettered individual judgment has been successfully denied in legal, moral and historical questions, but in which it has, none the less, survived, so far as purely deductive reasoning is concerned, within the shelter of apparently harmless mathematical studies.'[2]

4. On this new discipline Mr. C. B. Allen has made a number of fundamental observations which I have never seen better stated. He points out, what is obvious to statisticians but not to accountants, that 'statistical models rely to a great extent on that part of mathematics which concerns probability, normal distributions, and the like'. In my first lecture in this series I said that accounting dynamics was concerned with controlled and repeatable measurements of economic events, as they affect a particular entity, and their differences. Although for the most part accounts do pin us down to the facts, I think we should once again notice the general subconscious association in most people's minds of repetitive with expected. Mr. Allen says that: 'Any business organization is a group of related activities which can be expressed in a manner

[1] N.A.C.A. Bulletin, June, 1955, Section 1, p. 1333.

[2] *The Design of Experiments*, by R. A. Fisher (Oliver and Boyd Ltd., 1937). Second Edition, p. 10.

which will result in predictable patterns. There is enough "repetitiveness" in such an organization to make it possible to use the technique of mathematical models. By considered manipulation of the conditions, we can see how a business organization will change with varying circumstances.' Mr. Allen believes that most industrial accountants will find an application in their own companies. Among his several suggestions are cost and profit variation with volume, product mix for maximum profitability, inter-relationship of price-cost-profit, and marginal costs and revenues. I do not think it can be gainsaid, in Mr. Allen's words, that: 'Prediction is a necessary preliminary to decisions in business. We have been gathering bundles of statistics for a long time, without really bringing them to bear on company fortunes.'[1] The exercise of economic choice, the source of all reasonable decisions, depends upon a review of the expectations from a number of different uses of resources.

5. Mr. Allen draws attention to the detail making up the *operating structure* of the business world. He says, 'there is a lot of it handy but not in usable form. We must review it to remove all non-standard, erratic or just plain suspicious figures. To be useful, the raw data must be properly classified.'[2] Formal and logical classifications have been stressed in this series of lectures. His next points are vital ones. It *must* be recognized that models are only symbolic representations of the economic world. 'Models which are based on a presumption of permanent equilibrium and unvarying relationships will completely break down.' Nevertheless, a model is always a highly intense, inclusive, and abstract affair, but we should notice that, 'in model making, with its intense inclusiveness, we can begin to think in terms of an abstraction and its points of divergence from reality'.[3] This is clearly good mental discipline of a formalized order, requiring a fair knowledge of algebra, for it is in this department of mathematics that relationships are equated 'through numerical symbolism, to determine the unknown quantities from the known'.[4]

6. Before I have done with Mr. Allen's article I think it essential

[1] N.A.C.A. Bulletin, June, 1955, Section 1, pp.1321–2. [2] p. 1323.
[3] p. 1324. [4] p. 1325.

to give you his general rules in setting up and resolving a problem. I think they are excellent. Thus:

1. Go over the problem carefully, clarify the conditions and circumstances and eliminate anything not pertinent to it.
2. Set down the appropriate symbol or number for each relevant condition.
3. State the relationships or conditions in the form of equations. There should be as many equations as there are unknowns.
4. Solve the equations by algebra. Re-state the answer in the language of the problem.
5. Check the result to see that it complies with all conditions of the problem.[1]

Accountants of the future must be well versed in algebra, even to the extent of advanced forms like matrix algebra, if they are ever to come to grips with this model technique. But for some this may not seem so surprising. The real foundation for this kind of work so far as accountants are concerned, is the formal operating account as set in the logical structure of accounts which we are putting forward. The whole should be recognized as 'a very tight condensation of many factors and relationships. Separate models, or equations, can be established to make a further breakdown or analysis of each' aggregate category in the equations represented by the accounts themselves, and their interrelationships.

7. I add one last illustration. In the N.A.C.A. Bulletin on *Accounting for Research and Development Costs*[2] a reference is made to a paper presented by Mr. Ralph H. Manley at the fifth annual conference on industrial research held at Columbia University in 1954. The title of this paper was 'Translating Economic Aspects of Company Policy into Research Policy', and in it was described a technique for establishing the amount of a research appropriation and for determining how much to spend for different purposes. The point I want to bring out is the type of formula which was suggested. Thus:

[1] N.A.C.A. Bulletin, June, 1955, Section 1, p. 1327.

[2] The National Association of Cost Accountants, 505 Park Avenue, New York, 22 N.Y. Bulletin June, 1955, Section 3, Research Series No. 29.

To generalize, let

P=plant investment.
W=working capital.
R=research and development before taxes.
Y=recoupment period.
S=annual sales volume.
N=minimum acceptable net profit on sales.

Then
$$\frac{\dfrac{P+W+\dfrac{R}{2}}{Y}}{S}\times 100N.$$

And
$$R=2\,(0{\cdot}01YNS-P-W).$$

It is remarked that

such a formula is far from perfect. But if the relationships of sales volume to plant costs; to working capital; to minimum acceptable return on sales; and to the necessary payout period are all adjusted to the nature of the new business being considered, it does give research management a guide to the magnitude of allowable research and development costs.

An example is added in the following terms:

If 6 per cent is the acceptable rate of profit on sales, annual sales from a proposed new product are expected to be \$6,000,000, the investment required is estimated at \$1,500,000, and management desires to recover this investment in five years, the amount the company can afford to spend to develop the product is:

$$2(0{\cdot}06\times 5\times \$6{,}000{,}000-\$1{,}500{,}000)=\$600{,}000.^{1}$$

This is a means of determining the amount of a specially classified aggregate in an expectation account.

8. Once again, I remind you that the purpose of the main exercise is to establish a complete, simple and logical structure of accounts. I believe the general double-entry design put forward here is a *necessary* framework for the examination of particular correlations between aggregates. When carefully conceived in formal economic terms it becomes a rational scheme for interpreting conceptional relationships.

[1] *Op. cit.*, p. 1398.

9. In the theory of the firm, there is a point of view which suggests that more emphasis could usefully be put on particular decisions, and less on particular periods of time.[1] Although I pick this point out of its context, I sense an implied misunderstanding of accounting adaptability. Particular decisions involve results over time which must be formally accounted for if anything is to be learned about the consequences of those decisions, e.g. changes from expectations. Indeed, in my theory a particular *economic* decision would follow a review of a series of formal operating accounts which set out the *expected* results in both short- and long-term periods of a number of different known possibilities. The constraint of periodicity is surely inescapable.

10. There are one or two detailed points on the formal construction of the operating account with which I have been asked to deal. The first concerns the absence of a debit item for bad debts. I know that in the ordinary profit and loss accounts of firms this item is treated as an expense which is properly allowable for taxation purposes. But here the issue is different. We are concerned with a strictly theoretical account designed for interpretative purposes. A logical placing of categories is therefore important. I gave the clue to a strict theoretical treatment of bad debts in *Social Accounts and the Business Enterprise Sector of the National Economy*. There, I said that:

> The accounting process of writing off debts involves a downward adjustment to a former asset for debtors which is tantamount to a reduction in the circulating capital fund of the enterprise. Since movements of debtors and creditors, in fact all sector balance sheet items, must find their way into the resting account, the writing off of debts necessitates an entry in the resting account.[2]

Nowadays the name *capital change* account is preferred to resting account, but the implications are clear. Sales converted into

[1] Cf. *Industrial Efficiency and Growth*, by Charles Kennedy. Bulletin of the Oxford University Institute of Statistics, p. 56—footnote 2.

[2] University of Cambridge, Department of Applied Economics, Monograph 2 (Cambridge University Press, 1949), p. 70.

debtors become financial claims due to the enterprise. As such they are part of its capital structure. If they fail to be liquidated into cash they become capital losses chargeable as such in the capital change account. But this is not to say that capital losses are irrelevant to operating management. Capital losses are just as much a matter for management concern as operating expenses, and there are many instances of strictly theoretical capital losses necessarily incurred for trading purposes which are thereby properly allowable as charges against profits for taxation purposes.

11. Since my last lecture some of my friends have taken me to task for including depreciation of operating assets within the capital input as a fixed charge in the short period. I must, therefore, repeat the argument which I first used in *Precision and Design in Accountancy*,[1] although I had thought my general position was made plain in *Accounting Dynamics—II*. If it will bear repetition, I said that:

In the theory of product income presentation . . . , capital inputs have no part in work-in-progress valuations because they are regarded as standing charges or fixed expenses, thereby falling outside the make-up of the variable part of the operating account. This is consistent with the treatment followed in *Four Essays* where, it may be remembered, the total capital input was regarded as a fixed expense commitment because its component parts comprised rents (imputed or actual), depreciation of real assets and, for a strictly theoretical purpose, interest on *real* assets (excluding buildings because covered by rents) employed during the period of account. As Cameron has remarked in the special context of the production function, 'the plant-entity is usually associated with equipment and services whose rate of input is invariant over the entire range of the plant's output—or at least the relevant portion of its range. The function is defined with reference to these fixed inputs—which in practice mainly refer to investment goods and administrative services.' It follows that negative differences brought about by a comparison of the actual amounts of such fixed charges with the desirable levels determined by actual outputs, can be made to measure the ineffective surplus capacity effects of long-term errors in capital or asset formation.

[1] Gee and Co. (Publishers) Ltd., 1947.

It will be seen that Cameron stated the essential purpose of this discussion in the extract quoted. Later, at paragraph 17 in the same lecture, I said that

we are now at a stage in our product operating account when we may think of the relation between direct and ancillary labour . . . and net output as revealing an important production function, more particularly if we are prepared to regard the capital input as relatively fixed in the short period and entrepreneurial effort as similarly fixed.

And now for the argument as I stated it in *Precision and Design in Accountancy*. There I said

that it is possible to distinguish three major elements in those happenings which as related to assets, more particularly those classified as fixed, are covered by the accounting term depreciation. These elements may be conveniently expressed under the appellations of value, time and use. . .

i. VALUE: It is submitted that under this classification can be brought all external changes in values involving losses which ultimately tend to settle down to that position where they come to be regarded as relatively permanent, and which thereby lend themselves to some stability of measurement in money terms. Thus such a conception quite clearly takes in obsolescence.

ii. TIME: Any emphasis on time as an element in relation to depreciation is but a salutary reminder that all material things are transitory, a first principle we can never afford to neglect whatever our field of inquiry. Since they are not eternal all material things (which are very largely recognized in accounting terminology by qualification to the word assets) are subject to some measure of disintegration. Dawson, in his *Accountant's Compendium* (London, 1930) at p. 174, attempts a definition of the accounting term depreciation which includes a shrinkage in the cost price of value of any particular (physical) asset due to the mere effluxion of time. This comes very near to the conception which we are discussing, yet, although it may seem obvious it is desirable to distinguish between the actual temporal deterioration of a physical asset and its related fall in value since the latter is but the monetary measurement, in so far as this is practicable, of the former reality. We should also notice that this temporal deterioration is ordinarily marked by the characteristic of gradualness. It is not a jerky affair due to some special cause but a relatively smooth decline which may be reasonably looked upon as both natural and inherently inevitable; a character which should influence the basis of its measurement in money terms.

iii. USE. This conception relates depreciation to cost in proportion as physical asset resources are used in production. Thus, a physical asset at any particular point of time is regarded as a store of future production units. The using up of such units is measured in terms of a direct cost of production. In other words, depreciation is conceived as a productive exhaustion of usefulness. . . . It seems clear that . . . those cases falling within the first classification (i. VALUE) require to be measured in terms of the actual settled external fall in value, over the period of time during which that fall took place. Those cases coming within the second classification (ii. TIME) suggest a pronounced bias in favour of straight-line measurement, and it seems equally clear that those cases falling within the third classification (iii. USE) require a basis of measurement which is related to output, preferably in terms of production centres (cf. the familiar machine hour and labour hour rates).

I then proposed

that the practical problem concerning uniformity in the measurement of normal depreciation as specifically related to those fixed assets which are acquired for operational purposes, mainly lies in the reconciliation of two methods of calculation, one of which, having regard to the guiding canon which we have noticed, should have the pre-eminence. If this view is acceptable, the following basis of measurement suggests itself as a tentative solution.

(1) Ascertain the time period which under reasonably normal and settled conditions would represent the useful life of the operational asset to be depreciated.

(2) Estimate the normal productivity in terms of output of that asset over the time period ascertained under (1).

(3) Calculate the measure of depreciation on a straight-line basis having regard to *both* the factors in (1) and (2). It should be explained that the time factor in (1) will in reality be regulated by the output factor in (2) so that the actual arithmetical calculation of depreciation will be a simple one based on time. Having made this calculation it is important to realize that it is simultaneously related to normal output. The importance of this will be seen from the suggestions put forward at (4) and (5) below.

(4) Quicken the measure of depreciation above the straight-line calculation in proportion as output rises above the normal level estimated at (2), and retain this quickened basis during the time that productivity continues above normal.

(5) Do not slacken the measure of depreciation at any time below the straight-line calculation notwithstanding the circumstance that output may have fallen below the normal level—estimated at (2).

Some of you may remember that in an additional note I also drew attention to an article in the *Journal of Accountancy* for June, 1945 by E. L. Grant and P. T. Norton entitled 'An Engineering Viewpoint on Depreciation Accounting' in which a standard of comparison to test the adequacy of past depreciation charges was suggested in the following terms: '. . . past depreciation charges have been inadequate whenever the book value of an existing plant is higher than one could afford to pay for the existing plant in comparison with the most economical new plant.' I added the comment that this was a test to which I should wish to give consideration at accounting date intervals.

12. So much for the originating argument which really determines my treatment of depreciation in the formalized accounts put forward in these lectures. I know that some of you will feel that in this context I should again deal with the monetary measurement problems implicit in the reference to 'end-period prices' noted in *Four Essays* but I think enough was said there to keep me free on this score. What we are concerned with here is the positioning of the item. I think you will see from what has been said that I regard the time and normal output calculation as appropriate to the fixed short-period capital input. The increase occasioned by the quickened measure I should be willing to regard as a variable relateable to the accounting measurement of net output before the determination of the variable margin. Foreseen obsolescence I would bring within the time element, and unforeseen obsolescence within the value element. In *The Formal Principles of Public Company Accounting* I drew attention to the expedience of treating a 'provision for depreciation, renewals, or diminution in value of fixed assets' as an amount to be *charged to revenue*, thereby bringing an aggregate within the disclosure requirement of the

Companies Act, 1948, but I also said that in so far as there is any element of capital loss, it should be assigned, theoretically, to a capital change account. I suggested that the features of a capital loss, associated with a fixed asset, could be thought of in the following terms:

(*a*) Realization: The loss should be realized, or if unrealized in the sense that there has been no exchange transaction, the fixed asset source of the loss should be without value, and incapable of further use.

(*b*) Irregularity: The loss should be unforeseen and unexpected, uncertain and fortuitous, and therefore unallowed for.

I went on to say that it is sometimes said that obsolescence is always unforeseeable, but experience does not entirely support this view. Technological development in a quickly changing industry is to some extent expected, and in so far as this expectation can be imputed in accounting provisions, the resulting charges are properly treated as revenue inputs. In theory, at least, an unexpected loss due, for example, to sudden technological change should be treated as a capital loss, and disclosed in a capital change account. The make-up of the capital change account we shall come on to presently. I think there is little more that need be added now. It seemed necessary to repeat at length some of my earlier statements in order that the present positioning of the depreciation element of capital input in the present formalized accounts should be understood.

13. I now reproduce below a shortened narrative statement of the general form of operating account designed in accordance with some suggestions made to me by the late Mr. Philip Lyle. The purpose of this statement is to bring out a sharp measurement of the economic concept of net output, and to illustrate both its make-up and distribution. It will be clear to all accountants that this statement can be extended to include financial incomings and outgoings, United Kingdom taxation on profits, and dividend distributions, with retained income as a residue.

SHORTENED NARRATIVE STATEMENT OF OPERATING ACCOUNT.

1. GOODS and services purchased from outside. (Adjusted for changes in stocks, and the materials and direct expense contents of work in progress.)			
i. Raw materials		x	
ii. Manufacturing materials		x	
iii. Consumable tools		x	
iv. Purchased parts		x	
v. Carriage inwards		x	
vi. Fuel and Power		x	
vii. Commission work		x	
viii. Other direct expenses		x	
ix. Sale and distribution		x	
x. Standing overheads (including rents paid)		x	x
2. NET OUTPUT (the economic concept) or value added:			
i. Wages, salaries, national insurance and employees benefits of operative and ancillary labour (adjusted for change in the labour content of work in progress)	x		
ii. Wages, salaries, national insurance and employees benefits of sale and distribution	x		
iii. Wages, salaries, national insurance and benefits of administration and management	x	x	
iv. Imputed rents	x		
v. Depreciation of operating assets	x	x	
vi. OPERATING INCOME		x	x
GROSS OUTPUT			x
Value of Export sales		x	
Value of Home Trade sales		x	
		x	
Change in stocks of finished goods and finished parts		x	
GROSS OUTPUT		x	

14. In *Accounting Dynamics—II*, I set up a *product* operating account to give accounting measurements of net output and the

variable margin. In *Accounting Dynamics—III*, I set up the second part of a *general* form of operating account which began with a variable margin and ended up with a measurement of operating income. You will remember that it was concerned with the purchase of goods and services related to operating facilities and not ordinarily varying with output in the short period. It also had regard to wages, salaries, other remuneration and social insurance contributions allocated to standing overheads, and to administration and management. A final input dealt with capital and was composed of rents and the depreciation of operating assets, both thought of as reasonably invariant in the short period. Thus, this general form of account itemized the total operating overheads of the business entity or firm. The over-all relationship between the two forms of account I have mentioned can be established by inserting an intermediate account to assemble the net outputs and variable margins of the separate product, product group, or departmental operating accounts. The net output figures will be summarily noted and totalled in order to provide an over-all relationship between total operating overheads and total net outputs, for the reasons referred to in *Accounting Dynamics—III*. The total of the several variable margins will constitute the opening credit entry brought down to the general form of operating account dealing with operating overheads and the measurement of operating income.

15. If the analysis and allocation of operating overheads can be made deep enough there is, of course, no theoretical reason why a complete account down to the measurement of operating income should not be drawn for each product, product group or department. Indeed, in some cases pricing policies and control policies may require it. Nevertheless, a look at net outputs, variable margins and their changes, marshalled in one intermediate account, together with a study of the functions in the dependent separate accounts, should prove a reasonable enough guide for high executives who by the nature of their offices have not time for the investigation of too much accounting detail.

16. All proposed changes in the organization of a business entity should be accompanied by estimates of the related inputs and

outputs in financial terms. This is necessary in order that the financial improvement of the change may be reasonably judged. Moreover, the exercise of economic choice requires estimates of the financial prospects of alternative proposals. In a settled enterprise, I think that all estimates of this kind should take into account experienced relationships or functions which have come to notice in the accounts of past operations. That is to say standard relationships should be modified for proposed known changes to check the expected functions between estimated aggregates. In new enterprises working in an uncharted field much will depend upon immediate and actual patterns of change in relation to first empirical estimates, but in due time these relationships should settle down as the firm becomes more experienced in the ways of its general trend. Nevertheless, we should remember that no particular function, either standard or change, should be solely relied upon. It may be remembered that in *Design of Accounts* where only simple ratios were under consideration, the point was taken that 'any one ratio should not be too much relied upon in isolation—they should all be considered as contributing their part to any final interpretation of the accounting documents from which they were drawn.'[1] All accounting functions are interdependent as might be expected from the very nature of the double-entry system. Thus, as it seems to me, any quantitative theory of the firm must be finally deduced from a formal accounting pattern of interdependent relationships.

17. In the special context of some of the things we have been discussing in this series of lectures it is interesting to notice some points which have been made in the handbook put out by the Ministry of Agriculture and Fisheries on *The Farm as a Business.*[2] For example: 'There are two main types of budgetary analysis, known as partial and complete budgeting. In the former, estimates are made of the likely *changes* that will take place in a given organization if a suggested alteration is adopted. In the latter, the probable *total* costs and returns of a complete organization are studied.' Again: 'When the changes being considered are small

[1] Third edition 1949, p. 17.

[2] *A Handbook of Standards and Statistics for use in Farm Management Advisory Work.* H.M. Stationery Office 1954. (Reprinted 1955.)

relative to the whole . . . then only the variable costs need be considered. But when the alteration is a major one, then some of the items listed as fixed . . . will become variable.'[1] The last point which I want to bring to notice from this handbook is the straightforward statement that:

> To carry out a partial budget, four questions have to be answered:
> (*a*) What extra costs will arise?
> (*b*) What loss of present revenue will be incurred?
> (*c*) What saving in present costs will be made?
> (*d*) What extra revenue will be achieved?[2]

The emphasis here is plainly on expected changes.

18. In the interests of completeness, I turn to a question which concerns *calculated changes* in one or two cardinal aggregates in the formal operating account, and I especially wish to bring to notice the suggestions of my colleague, Mr. Bedford Smith, on price and volume reactions which were noted in *Accounting Research* for January, 1955. There he put forward some simple formulae to answer the questions:

> '(*a*) If the sale price of a product is lowered, what increase in volume must be obtained if profit is not to be affected? and
> (*b*) If the sale price of a product is increased, what decrease in volume can be permitted before profit is adversely affected?'

Thus, where

V=variable cost per unit of output,
N=number of output units,
S=selling price per unit of output,
S_1=percentage fall in selling price per unit,
S_2=percentage rise in selling price per unit,
N_1=percentage rise in output,
N_2=percentage fall in output,

[1] *Ibid.*, p. 39. [2] *Ibid.*, p. 40.

then in percentage terms:

'(a) if sale price is lowered, the increase in volume required to maintain profit may be expressed as

$$\frac{100SS_1}{S-V-SS_1}$$

and (b) if sale price is increased, the decrease in volume that can be permitted without involving some reduction of profit may be expressed as

$$\frac{100SS_2}{S-V+SS_2}.'$$

As Bedford Smith points out these formulae can be applied quite easily provided the normal selling price and the variable cost of production are known, but he adds a note of caution, to the effect that:

> These formulae apply only in the restricted circumstances that the required increase in volume can be supported without the incidence of increased *fixed* costs (i.e. that there is idle capacity available) and, alternatively that the indicated reduction in volume will *not* mean an increase in relatively fixed costs due to a change in cost categories (e.g. by the incidence of minimum wage provisions).

Bedford Smith goes on to remark that:

> The dual questions posed above have their corollary where it is desired to ascertain permissible changes in product sale prices consequent upon changed levels of output. . . . In percentage terms, . . . and subject to the limitations enumerated above, it will be seen that:
>
> (c) If output can be raised, product sale price may (without reducing profit) be reduced by
>
> $$\frac{100N_1(S-V)}{S(1+N_1)}$$
>
> and (d) If output falls, the consequent rise in sale price necessary to maintain the profit level may be expressed as
>
> $$\frac{100N_2(S-V)}{S(1-N_2)}.$$

These formulae also can be applied provided only that the normal selling price and the variable cost of production are known.

These formulae deal only with reciprocal movements in volume and price of the *same* product. It may be that it becomes necessary to reduce the selling price of one product merely to maintain sales equivalent to the existing output level. Then there may well be idle capacity, but this can be used only to increase the output of some other product. In these circumstances it becomes necessary to determine the level of volume increase required for the second product to offset the reduction in sale price of the first product. If we assume that:

	For the first Product.	*For the second Product.*
Normal selling price	S	T
Variable cost per unit of output	—	V_1
Normal output	N	O
Percentage fall in selling price	S_1	—
Percentage rise in output	—	O_1

Then the reduction in profit due to the fall in price of the first product is $N(SS_1)$
and the additional profit due to the increased output of the second product is $OO_1(T-V)$. . . .
In percentage terms, therefore, it may be said that, if the price of the first product is reduced in association with a steady volume of production and sales, then the increase in volume of production of a second product required to offset the loss so incurred is

$$\frac{100N(SS_1)}{O(T—V_1)}.$$

Once again, these formulae can be applied, within the limits outlined above, provided the essential data in regard to output levels, selling prices and variable costs are known.

19. While we are on this 'gathering-up' process of the relevant issues surrounding the formal operating account, I think we should notice that if we align the purchases and sales of goods and *outside* services in a product operating account with the originating sources of supply and demand then we get what is virtually an

input-output table for that particular product. I think a great deal could be gained from a study of the short period changes in such a table.

20. Our operating *change* account is designed to show relations between the rates of input factors and the rates of outputs, but these internal functions, as we know, are themselves dependent upon external functions (if they are determinable) of factor-supply and consumption. Cameron, it will be remembered, added a third which he called the entry function or normal profit condition.[1] In economic literature the general point of view taken in the theory of the firm is that where there are alternative courses of action, the expectations of which can be determined from these internal and external functions, then choice should be exercised where the maximum profit lies. Equilibrium is the keynote. Accordingly, Cameron is able to say, '. . . if the steel industry finds that its stocks of steel for sale are either rising or falling, then it is not in equilibrium'.[2] This type of test can be applied not only to an industry but also to a firm in order to judge whether the firm is in equilibrium with its own industry.

21. There are two other points, one specific and one general, which I should wish to take from Cameron. The first concerns a particular operating overhead. Thus, '. . . practical experience suggests that entrepreneurial effort by nature approximates rather to a variable input—the volume of planning, directing and co-ordinating staff being increased with the level of activity'.[3] This is plainly something which does happen and which should be detectable from the internal sequential relationships between the specific overhead for administration and management and net outputs. This sectional behaviour relationship is determinable from the general part of the formal operating account and the suggested intermediate account which gathers up the net outputs of the separate product operating accounts. The second and general point implies quite simply that it is only by examining movements (i.e. *changes*) that we can appreciate the effect of 'substitution or economizing decisions'.[4]

[1] *The Determination of Production*, by Burgess Cameron (Cambridge University Press, 1954). [2] *Ibid.*, p. 7. [3] *Ibid.*, p. 23. [4] *Ibid.*, p. 30.

22. In the theory of the firm marginal cost is simply the increase in total costs divided by the *increased* units of production. We know that fixed costs per unit of product always fall with increases in volume. Variable costs usually rise when increased units of labour are associated with temporarily fixed capital equipment. Eventually the increase in variable costs will offset the fall in fixed costs. Thus, in order to maximize profits, production should be increased all the time that marginal revenue is larger than marginal cost. The optimum is reached when marginal cost is equivalent to marginal revenue. Hence, the importance of investigations into *changes* quantified in accounts.

23. In our general understanding of change accounts, internal functions constitute a study of the behaviour of different items of expenditure in relation to outputs, as opposed to cost control which involves the classification of expenditure into groups according to where the responsibility lies and dealing with necessary expenditures at different levels of activity.

24. It is frequently asserted, and I believe true, that normal functional relationships should exist between various kinds of investment and output. Unfavourable relationships between real investment and the volume of business done should show themselves from comparisons between net outputs and standing charges, and their changes. If we could measure the normal proportion of equilibrium net output properly to be given up to standing charges, then the difference between this figure and *actual* standing charges would measure either exceptional effectiveness or the ineffectiveness of surplus capacity.

25. We are, therefore, very much concerned with the full and effective use of short-run costs and that opportunities for profit should not be neglected by their under-utilization. When we come to look at our several product operating accounts the last pound sterling spent on any one product operation should not yield less output than it would yield if applied to some other product. Thus, variable resources should be so combined in an enterprise plan that each will be earning at its optimum rate. Clearly then, the productivity of variable resources will raise the productivity of fixed resources. We should, therefore, seek to combine with

fixed resources as large a quantity of variable resources as can be profitably employed.

26. Change expectations are concerned with decisions in the present about variations in future inputs and outputs. Specific expectations are always marred by some uncertainties, and they must be assessed against general background expectations about income, investment, savings, employment, consumers' spending, exports and imports, and government policies. Specific expectations peculiar to the firm are taken up with relative costs, relative prices, the presence of competitors and product demands. If a firm is monopolistic enough to regard all the relevant variables as sufficiently within its own control and knowledge, then it can forecast with some confidence. Nevertheless, large monopolistic undertakings with large investment do sometimes sacrifice the quality of flexibility inseparable from economic choice.

27. In my first lecture in this series, I said that changes in accounting aggregates could be formally classified in three ways. First, the plain and straightforward differences between the actual figures of two accounting periods, sequential or otherwise. Second, the variances between empirically predetermined standard and actual figures which have become so familiar in the methods of cost accounting. Third, the differences between expected changes and realized changes. Enough has been said both here and in the available literature on the first two classifications. We are left with the third. Accordingly, I think it should be possible to construct an operating change account on formal lines contrasting expected changes, based on experienced standard relationships adjusted for currently known expected deviations, with actual changes. Short-period historical accounts of this nature should immediately bring to notice unsuspected exogenous variables which promote the factual results of uncertainties. By this means experience may be gained of the behaviour of unknowns.

28. There is always a need for a study of change accounts for in practice neither marginal revenues nor marginal costs can be readily determined from the ordinary run of financial accounts which only tend to deal in total aggregates and the expression of trends as averages. Moreover, in a formal operating account,

outgoings should always be sub-classified, in so far as this is possible, according to *experienced* variability, and this is the real way to deal with that nebulous so-called 'Semi-variable' category of outgoings. If an expense is fixed for an X level of output but variable at an X_1 level of output, then it becomes variable at $X_1 - X$ levels of outputs and this should show itself in the operating change accounts. Again, and in a different context, the effects of factor substitution will always show themselves in the operating change accounts. There can be no doubt of the importance of these accounts. The full employment of fixed assets is eventually detectable from the relation between capital inputs, and net outputs. In the appropriation account financial income is directly relateable to financial investment, and when we come to such matters as social accounting it is easy to see the significance of consumption and savings functions in the outlay account when these are considered in relation to a general asset background. For example, it has always seemed to me that a saving/spending relationship with income and assets is of fundamental importance in understanding the desired behaviour of a national economy.

29. And so I pass from a firm entity to a national entity and back again to a firm entity, and I add that when considering relatively long-term changes I still have respect for the time-honoured method of moving totals. Thus, it is said that a better picture of the trend of the activities of a business and its several departments, can be obtained by plotting the totals of twelve successive monthly periods instead of the individual monthly figures. As each month's figure comes up it is added to the last annual total and the figure for the corresponding month in the previous year is deducted. As a consequence, the new annual total gives the total for twelve months ending with the current month. It thus takes in all variations due to stoppages, seasonal fluctuations and so on. The moving annual total thereby gives a steady and reasonable guide to the general trends of business.

30. Accounts can be made to provide the data for future management needs, but the accountant should never forget the probable importance of so-called 'lost-opportunity' costs. These

might be collected with advantage as occasion offers, for in this way management decisions could be scientifically studied.

31. Change is complex and as much qualitative as quantitative. For this reason, I have become sceptical of systems of accounting which seek to set back present results and specific aggregates in terms of base period equivalents. I think the implications of quantitative change are best dealt with at the close of short-period accounts, because standard and change relationships then become relevant within short-term periodic frameworks. Thus, I think general aggregate measures are best set back in general monetary or price-level terms. In a later lecture, I shall pass on to a strict analysis of the capital change account.

7

BASIC CONCEPTS IN ACCOUNTING—

ECONOMIC ACCOUNTING: A STUDY IN CONCEPTIONAL RELATIONSHIPS

The substance of papers given to the Annual Conference of the Association of Incorporated Statisticians at Balliol College, Oxford, on 17th September, 1955, and to the National Conference of the British Institute of Management at Harrogate in November, 1955

1. I understand that this conference is concerned with the contribution of science to the future management of enterprise, and I have been asked to deal with those ideas in accounting, economics and mathematical statistics which may show themselves to be relevant to the general development of that contribution. I suppose when most business executives talk about this kind of thing they usually think in terms of the physical, natural and mechanical sciences, whereas I shall have to try and deal with my subject from a standpoint within the social sciences. There is a feeling in the business world that social science is vague and inexact, incapable of controlled experiment, and when it tries to be precise its exponents wrap themselves up in a mass of unintelligible patterns and symbols.

2. This puts me at a disadvantage, for whereas most business-men have come to see that research ideas in the physical, natural and mechanical sciences can become eventually matters of vital concern if firms are to keep their places in the ever-changing orders of industry, they are sceptical of the usefulness of applied economic fancies and their accounting derivatives in the management of enterprise. The first set of ideas is better understood because it anticipates change at the points where it is most required in terms of profit and loss. Improved technical methods of production economize in the use of materials, labour and capital; improved and varied products promote stability and better revenues. The second set of ideas is largely interpretative of what

is supposed to be happening and what might happen. There is room for much opinion on what is already past history, and future notions are notoriously speculative; all too frequently a complicated statistical exercise seems only to confirm what common sense already knew.

3. Nevertheless, as it seems to me, there is always a real need for logical interpretations of the facts which industry day by day collects and records in systems of accounting. Interpretations are unlikely to be logical if they are not based on scientific principles. First and foremost I am an accountant and what I shall have to say will be coloured by that background, but perhaps I should make it clear that I do not propose to deal with cost controls or technical cost saving devices in the way of operations and methods; these subjects are wearing a little thin by much overwork in management discussions. And neither shall I claim any special knowledge of mathematical statistics, for that must be left to the econometricians to support, but I shall treat of the study of accounting from a scientific rather than a juristic point of view; and for this purpose I shall wish to regard it as having something in common with mathematics much in the manner that some medieval exponents of double entry treated it, and as I am now told so did Jeremy Bentham. It was not an accident that early ideas about accounting appeared in mathematical treatises. So, too, I shall justify the ideas of what is really a technical exercise in the social sciences on the same plane of reference. Before I become pronouncedly practical, as I know you will wish me to be, perhaps you will let me quote from the works of a very old writer[1] who saw with amazing clarity the place in the scheme of things of the second set of ideas to which I referred in the previous paragraph. These quotations are long, but I think worth giving, and you may skip them if you wish. Thus:

A definition that concentrates on pure form belongs rather to logic than to natural science. A definition about material conditions without reference to form could come only from physics, for it takes a physicist to deal with matter like that. Nevertheless a definition covering what is

[1] *Philosophical Texts*, selected and translated by Thomas Gilby (Oxford University Press, 1951), Science and Wisdom Nos. 52–55.

from both: namely matter and form, has a more authentic ring of natural science.

Some sciences are intermediate between physics and mathematics. They accept purely mathematical propositions and apply them to sensible matter. In musical theory, for instance, arithmetical reflections on numerical proportions are turned to sound.

Thus, a musical notation is in one sense an account with properties of structure and form. And now for the hub of the present matter:

Accidents arrive in the following sequence. First quantity, afterwards quality, then transmutation and change. Hence, quantity can be conceived as investing substance without implying sensible qualities. Its meaning does not depend on sensible but on intelligible matter. When accidents are removed, the naked substance can be grasped only by the mind. The senses cannot reach it. The mathematician deals with such abstractions as quantities and their consequences: namely figures and so forth.

And to close these pertinent quotations:

Mathematical demonstrations are analytic and explicate the formal cause, but when, as in the natural sciences, the proof proceeds by outside causes, a peculiarly rational measure is set: namely the discursive process from one object to another. Hence it has been remarked how the ratiocinative process is appropriate to natural science, not exclusively, but as being most strongly emphasized there. In much the same way the didactic process is appropriate to mathematics, for we are said to proceed didactically when our argument is purely deductive.

4. I have no doubt that in any other place and at any other time, perhaps in this place and time, most of my present auditors would regard the proffer of these quotations as unnecessarily pedantic, but I have to remind you that we are concerned with a department of social science and the impact of its method on the future management of enterprise. I have always wanted to regard an account as a logical ordering of facts, but, as you will have judged this requires some attention to structure and form. So far, and in fact, accounting has been very much a utilitarian exercise

engaged in as evidence of stewardship. Moreover, as I noted once before,

> profits or enterprise income and financial solvency are major considerations in the conduct of any business. Profits are taxed, part distributed, and part saved, so that a fair accounting measure over time is a matter of consequence to all *entrepreneurs*. Apart from taxation, undistributed profits have become important indicators of the stabilizing and developing powers of business enterprises. The continuing ability to earn profits is still regarded as a criterion of effectiveness and a guarantor of capital values.

But here the issue is a different one. We shall make it our concern to look for a logical structure of accounts, as well as logical forms of accounts based on logical categories of recorded data ordered and set up by a scale of measurement which will bring them within a unified plane of reference. And we shall do this because we believe that past behaviour is a guide to probability, and correlations between logical aggregates are standards whereby to judge the coming results of future performances as and when they occur.

5. If all this is rightly conceived, logical simplicity in both structure and form is essential to the preparation of those accounting and statistical statements which are primarily organized for the understanding of enterprise leaders. Certainly they do not want to be weighed down by a mass and variety of heavily analysed material expressed in the stilted style of an ever-changing technical terminology: this seldom makes for valid interpretations of past behaviour. A main board requires simple, clear, and orderly forms which can be quickly assimilated and understood. Its members want to know about upward and downward trends in activity; whether or not they are peculiar to their own enterprise. Are there external factors causing disruption over the industry as a whole? If so, how can they be countered? What are the expectations of the future and so on? Right policies depend upon right answers to these questions.

6. A startling development in our generation has been the

steady furtherance of mechanized recording until we are now at a stage in the electronic processing of originating data. Thus, a mechanical science is serving a social science. Nevertheless, it is a matter of supreme importance that we should see this in its proper setting. Whatever mechanical aid is brought to the processing of originating data it will always lie in the range of the routine and regular transaction, and cannot be pushed much beyond it. Accordingly, if electronic aids are to give their maximum usefulness to business firms, everything will depend upon the final structure, and the form of the conceptual aggregates, of those accounting and statistical statements to which we have referred. You cannot frequently displace and change such a mechanistly ordered programme without great mischief. Indeed it could be a costly business. Invariance is the key-note and this imposes a rigorous compulsion. Necessity requires that the final outcomes shall be logically conceived so as to provide the best, and reasonably secure, interpretative means open to management. I was going to say reasonably permanent but that is too advanced a vision. This is a discipline of science and it will need much thinking to achieve it.

7. At this stage it might be well to ask a pertinent question. Where and to whom do we turn for information about conceptual aggregates which are likely to be logically interrelated in such a way as to yield reasonably valid inferences about a firm's affairs? I know that among businessmen I shall be in some danger in suggesting an answer, for I want to say that we should have a look at the ideas of those people who have taken time away from the world of business to think about its affairs. I say this because I think the ultimate long-term regulators appropriate to business management may be found in the practical adaptation of fundamental ideas rather than in a slavish attachment to those utilitarian principles which common sense is immediately likely to suggest from a necessarily surface regard of day-to-day problems. I believe it is well known that fundamental ideas in the physical and mechanical sciences usually spring from research which is undertaken apart from, and so not caught up in, the immediate day-to-day problems of applications. No doubt both are complementary

but there is a need for independent thinking, especially in our present field of inquiry. On the other hand we must be on guard against over-confidence, and we should not overlook what I regard as a special warning from a great economist. In his preface to the first edition of the *Principles of Economics*, Alfred Marshall[1] said:

> There has always been a temptation to classify economic goods in clearly defined groups, about which a number of short and sharp propositions could be made to gratify at once the student's desire for logical precision, and the popular liking for dogmas that have the air of being profound and are yet easily handled. But great mischief seems to have been done by yielding to this temptation, and drawing broad artificial lines of division where nature has made none. The more simple and absolute an economic doctrine is, the greater will be the confusion which it brings into attempts to apply economic doctrines to practice, if the dividing lines to which it refers cannot be found in real life.

8. The ideas which I am now going to put before you are very much in keeping with what I have been told to do in this paper. They largely derive from the development of social accounting, a subject which seems in parts to have brought accountants, economists and econometricians together. I opened a recent paper with what might seem a rather odd comment, when I said that I approached the subject of social accounting from the standpoint of an accountant. If it should seem strange that such a statement is necessary on a subject which includes accounting as one of its terms, then I must reply that, in fact, the modern idea of accounting for society began in the field of applied economics. This, of itself, should serve to show us that the basic concepts of economics and accounting are not so different.

Although, as you will have gathered, I now regard accountancy as more of a science than an art, and this is a minor reservation to what follows, nevertheless in a paper of this kind I think you should hear somebody on the other side of the fence to myself, who

[1] p. ix.

has only just recently had something to say on the issues I am now discussing. It will not then be thought that I am claiming too much for my own particular subject. Professor Fogarty[1] puts the matter shortly and simply thus:

Economics . . . is the study of social relationships in so far as they 'can be brought into relation with the measuring rod of money'. That is, economics is the science of which accountancy is the art. But it is only in very recent years that the two have joined forces. Till within the last generation the field of monetary analysis could be pictured as a large sheet of blotting paper, with an inkspot in each corner. One represented the economist, formulating hypotheses about monetary relationships in the market, or between nations, or between employers and workers; but having very little in the way of actual accounts against which to test them. The other represented the accountant, grappling with the actual financial records of business and the public service, but in the light of day-to-day needs, and without much concern for wider or longer-term hypotheses; for scientific analysis or reflection on the material on which he worked. The two spots spread gradually, putting out feelers towards one another. But only in the last ten years have they begun to coalesce really rapidly, and this has been due very largely to the appearance on the paper of a third spot, falling precisely between the first two. This represents social accounting, the analysis of the accounts of the whole economy, of a region, nation, or international group. Social accounting has come to the fore because, like business accounting, it serves urgent practical needs. It necessarily makes use . . . of the techniques and concepts of business and public authorities' accounting as already established. But it has been created for the most part by economists to answer the questions posed in economic hypotheses. In this field the accountant and the economist have had perforce to lie down together, and have ended by each discovering that the other is not bad company after all.

I take the matter a stage further, again using Professor Fogarty's[2] words:

It is an accident of history that econometrics is new, whereas the technique of accountancy is long established. When the logic of the two is

[1] *Economic Control* (London: Routledge and Kegan Paul, 1955), p. 247.
[2] *Ibid.*, 254.

argued out, it is clear that the econometrician and the accountant are doing the same thing. They each start from a problem ('How is the business to earn a profit?'—'How will purchase tax affect the demand for cotton piece-goods?'). They formulate, explicitly or implicitly, a hypothesis ('that consumers react to a change in price in a certain way': 'that the business, by proceeding on the lines followed in the last financial year, earns a profit'). They define the relevant variables, and design a system of money accounts to bring out not only the extent to which the hypothesis as a whole is, in fact, fulfilled (financial accounting) but (costing, standard costing) the influence of each variable on it. They then use the results for prediction, as a pointer to further variables which might be examined, or to throw up alternative hypotheses on which the problem might be more effectively solved. Econometrics is in principle simply the formal mathematical expression of the economic logic which runs through business accounts as well. It is the experimental, pioneering fringe of the art whose established procedures the accountant applies. In the newer development of accountancy the two meet.

At last someone else has had the courage to say these things, and the derivation of my present suggestions could not have been more plainly put.

9. If we keep clear of overmuch theory the immediate question of structure need not detain us very long. There are two simple propositions which essentially inform the structure of accounts of any entity, whatever that entity may be. The entity could be a firm, a person, a partnership, a company, a group of companies, an industry, a region, a nation, or an international group of nations. The two propositions depend upon the general economic concepts of periodic income and of wealth. The first says that in a given time period income is devoted to consumption expenditure and saving. The second says that saving is resolved in capital formation. We seldom find that companies and suchlike enterprises constituted for profit come within the ranks of final consumers. If we rule out consumption expenditure from the general run of business accounting, we are left with concepts of income, saving and capital. A proper accounting structure for a commercial enterprise, therefore, will be generally expressed in a set of formally related accounts; an operating or profit and loss account

to measure period income from economic activity, an appropriation account to show transfers of income and the measurement of saving, a capital change account centred around the application of saving, and a balance sheet to measure capital as a stock and to record its make-up constants and variants.

10. When considering the form of accounts we have first to deal with primary accounts and the relationships between the aggregate categories included in those accounts. By so doing we form a judgement on past behaviour. Thereafter we have to look at difference or change accounts and the relationship between the aggregate categories included in those accounts in order to form a judgement on probable behaviour. In setting up these accounts we should concentrate on clear and simple forms, so that categories for aggregates are few, conceptually derived, logically related, and essential. In this way their significance can be quickly taken in and understood.

11. Form in a mathematical exercise is a matter of the equivalence of reduced symbols. Similarly, form in the accounting exercise is always a matter of the equivalence of symbolic aggregates expressing measurements of logical concepts. An account based on the principle of double entry must inherently recognize and portray the constraint of equivalence and that is why, given logical connotations of accounting variables, their behaviour relationships over time should be capable of mathematical expression. If we can limit or minimize, that is, significantly reduce, the number of variables with precise connotations formally arranged in an account, it should make for clarity and understanding.

12. Form and behaviour, then, so far as executive boards are concerned, very largely resolve themselves in a 'tidying-up' of the layout of a few familiar accounts which constitute the structure to which we have referred. Measurement problems will be touched upon when and where they are relevant, but since the issues which they involve are well known, little that is new can be added here.

13. We shall begin with a form of operating account designed to measure *inter alia* net output and operating income. Such an

account is inadequate for management purposes unless it also records the changes from one accounting period to another (both sequential and comparable where expected differences are in point), between significant aggregates capable of being correlated within the logical framework of the whole structure of accounts. The aggregates themselves (that is, the accounting classifications) must be representative measurements of concepts which have a natural bearing on one another. Unexpected changes which affect firms should be detected immediately they arise and for this reason the preparation of short-period operating accounts which mark immediate differences in behaviour is essential. Similarly devised long-period operating accounts also have their uses for the observance of long-term changes in trends. The preparation of all such accounts can be either all-embracing of the economic activities of the firm, or, if needs be, limited to special products, groups of products, departments and sometimes processes.

14. In a recent research lecture[1] I suggested that change relationships could emphasize marginal efficiencies, and I put the question: Are these relationships improving or falling back on those already established as standard? Standard referred both to the type of relationship and its experienced measure. I also suggested that at the level of general policy-making such relationships should influence decisions. Thus, accounts designed on a simple formal basis to reveal logically dependent aggregates, and their changes from one accounting period to another, may tell a better and more easily assimilated story than some other designs based on the estimates of cost controls. Changes in short-term operating accounts should give us short-term accounting information about incremental costs and revenues and so enable us to observe the behaviour of costs with changes in outputs. Accordingly, such bilateral marginal relationships should give us the results of expansionist or contractionist policies and assist us to arrive at the short-term equilibrium position of the firm. The source of these ideas is still Marshall on increments,

[1] *Accounting Dynamics—III.*

for in his preface to the eighth edition of the *Principles of Economics*, he said very pointedly that

variations in the nature of marginal costs are indeed largely responsible for the well-known fact that those effects of an economic cause, which are not easily traced, are frequently more important than, and in the opposite direction to, those which lie on the surface and attract the eye of the casual observer. This is one of those fundamental difficulties which have underlain and troubled the economic analysis of past times; its full significance is perhaps not yet generally recognized, and much more work may need to be done before it is fully mastered.

In the context of our present discussion I think we should especially notice his next paragraph.

The new analysis is endeavouring gradually and tentatively to bringover into economics, as far as the widely different nature of the material will allow, those methods of the science of small increments (commonly called the differential calculus) to which man owes directly or indirectly the greater part of the control that he has obtained in recent times over physical nature. It is still in its infancy; it has no dogmas, and no standard of orthodoxy. It has not yet had time to obtain a perfectly settled terminology; and some differences as to the best use of terms and other subordinate matters are but a sign of healthy life. In fact, however, there is a remarkable harmony and agreement on essentials among those who are working constructively by the new method; and especially among such of them as have served an apprenticeship in the simpler and more definite, and therefore more advanced, problems of physics. Ere another generation has passed, its dominion over that limited but important field of economic inquiry to which it is appropriate will probably be no longer in dispute.

15. Behaviour relationships of another order and with a different mathematical significance can be derived between variable balance sheet aggregates and operating account aggregates, e.g. standard inventories and gross outputs, liquid balances and total transactions, debtors and sales, and creditors and purchases. I think there is some evidence for thinking that these may turn out to be log-normal relationships, and I have discussed some of the implications in my third research lecture on *Accounting Dynamics*.

I think it is reasonably clear that standard behaviour relationships are bound to show up in the logically constructed accounts of a business which has been successfully continued on a more or less even keel. My general point is, therefore, that we can regard all the various kinds of relationships between accounting aggregates which we have touched upon as giving a complete, balanced and constrained view of the transactions of a business which is in a state of effectiveness. As I have remarked, we continually need to ask ourselves whether these formal patterns and their consequential relationships can be held taut in the required order of a perfect use of resources.

We have also to think of accounting increments beyond the immediate bilateral requirements of short-term equilibrium, and regard them as a practical means of relating income and capital changes over time in order that we may look for some backward and forward relationships in a general pattern of change. Indeed, it may very well turn out that change accounts are the vital link between historical accounting and expectation accounting.

In these exercises we are all the time seeking for some universal principles by which to gauge the effective use of resources by a firm.

16. This kind of work can be greatly extended and you may be interested to know about a paper by J. S. Cramer and H. Theil of the Central Planning Bureau, The Hague, *On the Utilization of a New Source of Economic Information.* This paper was presented at the European meeting of the Econometric Society which took place in Uppsala in August, 1954. It dealt with a survey (to be called Munich Business Test)

> based on monthly reports of *entrepreneurs* about the direction of change of a large number of micro variables.

The analysis reported in the paper referred to

> six branches of the German leather and shoe industry . . . and most of them cover the period February, 1951 to November, 1953.

It seems from the report of the Uppsala meeting prepared by Bent Hansen and published in *Econometrica* for April, 1955 that

for each branch of industry, for each variable and in each month, the proportions of firms reporting a rise, a fall, and no change are calculated, the individual answers being weighted according to the size of the firms.

As a first approach to the data we are told that

it seems possible to analyse the degree of conformity of behaviour and anticipations among separate firms of the same branch. For this purpose, monthly *disconformity coefficients* have been computed, for each variable and for each branch of industry. These coefficients give some insight into the empirical applicability of the theoretical concept of a homogeneous industry. It appears that there are rather substantial differences between the individual anticipations and still larger differences among the actual outcomes.

It is also interesting to learn that

the second approach followed deals with the familiar econometric problem of establishing, testing, and eliminating relationships between economic variables. For this purpose, monthly balances of the separate variables have been used. Such a balance is defined as the difference between the proportion of firms reporting an increase and that of firms reporting a decrease. These balances may be regarded as measures of central tendency of the individual changes of the variables and anticipations of separate firms.

I think we can see that this type of survey might well be adapted to data derived from firms' analyses of change based on their accounts in the manner we are proposing. This could prove a big step forward in the statistical needs of various branches of industry.

Price changes are also important because we learn from the survey already referred to that

> it appears . . . the selling prices of the four trade branches, both actual and planned, are mainly determined by the buying prices (actual and expected, respectively) of the same month. No influence of buying prices of previous months can be detected. Neither is it possible to find any systematic influence of other possibly relevant variables, such as stocks and turnover.

The latter comment is surprising.

17. I now turn to the detailed order of a firm's accounts. As promised, I start with the operating account and view it in three sections. The first is primarily concerned with conceptual measurements of gross and net outputs. I regard net output as the fundamental concept because it measures value added by the organization and utilization of the factors of production in operating activity. In the theory of the firm I think it a central concept and one which cannot be discarded. You are no doubt familiar with its use for census purposes and you will recognize its relevance to the development of input-output analysis. Therefore, we may regard this concept as the real peg on which a firm can fasten its own accounts and make them conformable with external statistics. By so doing it should be able to interpret its own accounts the more readily, against a wide background of national statistics. For example, if the Census of Production is treated as a basic structure, no matter how historical that structure may be thought, it can always be judged as a starting-off point. Standard relationships can be calculated for one's own branch of industry at this juncture and compared with those shown by one's own accounts for the same period. Changes will show in subsequent periodic change accounts to enable managements to judge improvements or recessions. Thus, census figures can be treated by business managements as over-all basic checks on general average trends to test their own showings, and if need be to pull their own standards into line at the regular intervals of published official data.

18. I set out the first section of the operating account in the following manner:

OPERATING ACCOUNT

	Period 1	Period 2	Change		Period 1	Period 2	Change
2. GOODS purchased (originating and intermediate), adjusted for changes in stocks and the materials content of work-in-progress	x	x	x	1. GROSS OUTPUT, i.e. sales of finished goods and finished parts, adjusted for change in stocks ...	x	x	x
3. OUTSIDE services (originating and intermediate), adjusted for change in direct expense content of work-in-progress ...	x	x	x				
4. GOODS and outside services purchased in connection with the sale and distribution of finished goods and finished parts, adjusted for change in stocks (if any)	x	x	x				
	—	—	—				
5. TOTAL consumption of goods and services varying with output	x	x	x				
6. THE ACCOUNTING MEASUREMENT OF NET OUTPUT or value added ...	x	x	x				
	—	—	—		—	—	—
	x	x	x		x	x	x
	═	═	═		═	═	═

19. In *Accounting Dynamics—II*, I placed in this section of the operating account the detailed items that I should expect to find within the classification of goods purchased and outside services. Thus, in goods purchased I included raw materials, manufacturing materials, consumable tools and purchased parts, and under outside services I brought in carriage inwards, power, commission work and other direct expenses. There are one or two awkward

valuation problems to be noticed in this first section of the operating account if we are to derive strict relationships from its form. In theory, the adjustment for the change in stocks of finished goods and finished parts should be valued in accordance with selling prices and similarly the changes in the materials inventories should be valued at or near the last cost,[1] but I recognize the practical difficulties.

20. The category aggregate for gross output in the first section of the operating account is made up of sales of finished goods and finished parts, adjusted for the change in stocks of finished goods and finished parts. It is important to notice that this attempts a precise definition of gross output where manufacturing operations are in point, because it limits it to saleable products, and saleable implies value in exchange on a market.

21. In the first section of our operating account we are concerned with the measurement of changes in the make-up of an accounting view of net output. One of the primary functions to be derived from this section is that which bilaterally relates the operating consumption of goods purchased (originating and intermediate) to gross output. For the benefit of my cost accountant colleagues I should perhaps make clear an assumption that the material control procedures of cost accounting practice have looked after the technical job of preventing waste and ineffective usage. In the absence of special circumstances I should expect this function to be a constant, and, similarly, I should expect a function based on the changes in these aggregates from one accounting period to another to be a constant of the same order. Interfering special circumstances might be occasioned by price changes, or by technological improvements in the method or instruments of production involving economy in materials usage. If such influences and their effects are known, the expected alteration in the function is also known. That is to say, it becomes a new or revised constant. It will be remembered that throughout this formal accounting analysis we are looking for functional relationships between logical accounting aggregates as well as

[1] See the discussion in Appendix II of my monograph on *Social Accounts and the Business Enterprise Sector of the National Economy* (Cambridge University Press, 1949).

patterns of change relationships. A second function would relate the consumption of outside services acquired to gross output and a third, and rather obvious, function would relate goods and outside services purchased in connection with the sale and distribution of the product to gross output. All of these functions could be localized or narrowed down to a series based on particular categories of goods and outside services purchased and consumed, if past behaviour experience showed such relationships to be peculiarly significant. A study of the changes in such types of relationships would be valuable. In *Accounting Dynamics—II*, I said:

> A fall in the ratio of materials consumption to gross output might be directly relateable to a positive change in a particular part of the asset (capital) formation of a preceding or earlier period. An increase in the ratio of materials consumption to gross output is a matter for investigation if it cannot be ascribed to price. The consumption of outside services, however, may take on some of the characteristics of a factor supply. Thus, a positive change in some one service may give either an increasing or decreasing return. And so it becomes clear that the essential point is to study the related effect of changes on both sides of the account, and to judge whether a change in output has compensated for related changes in input. The more constant is the ratio of changes in total goods and services consumed to changes in gross output, the more significant becomes the relation between net output and factor inputs to be dealt with in the second and third parts of the product operating account, for then changes in net output are pointers to the marginal products of varied factor inputs.

In all this I think it especially desirable to point out that these change relationships may neither necessarily nor immediately appear between the changes of the same time period. They may very well hold between the changes of different time periods, so that a change in one aggregate may very well be related to a *latent* change in another aggregate. Experience should tell us this, but the great purpose of these *expected* relations is to put us on inquiry if no such actual relationships show themselves.

22. It may be well to reiterate the purpose of this analysis. What we are doing is to look for functional behaviour relationships

between logical accounting aggregates, especially patterns of change relationships. I do not know that such an approach can be properly regarded as new. What can be said is that accounting is at last taking steps to re-order its exercise in terms of scientific concepts derived from economics. It was in 1925 that Gustav Cassel[1] said:

Decisive importance attaches to the quantitative method in all investigations of dynamic conditions. Such investigations . . . must always begin by drawing up the normal curve representing the uniform development. When this is done, the actual movements can be measured as deviations from the normal curve. In such questions we can never be satisfied with qualified reasoning.

We can transform this idea into uniformity in behaviour relationships and the same principles should prevail whether the subject of our investigation be a firm or a nation. Cassel[2] also said, as it seems to me with much point, that:

A thorough reconstruction of economics as a quantitative science is urgently needed. . . . The aim of the reconstruction must be to present the actual facts and problems of economic life in the most distinct form and, as far as possible, in measurable terms.

This is surely the accounting task. But as if to show us the importance of right concepts within a right framework, Cassel[2] also uttered this warning:

Almost every author thinks himself entitled to build his theoretical concepts upon his own subjectively, and often rather casually, chosen concepts. Moreover, the quantitative fixation of the different concepts is for the most part lacking in precision. There is in economics much vague talk about 'quantities' without sufficient care being taken to ascertain that the concepts concerned can really be defined as quantities and are capable of being measured in definite units. These serious shortcomings do not prevent authors with some superficial knowledge of mathematics from representing such concepts by mathematical

[1] *Fundamental Thoughts in Economics* (London: Ernest Benn, 1925), p. 31,

[2] *On Quantitative Thinking in Economics* (Oxford, Clarendon Press, 1935), pp. v, 6.

symbols and using those symbols in all sorts of formulae and calculations. Great authority is claimed for conclusions drawn from these operations, but it is not realized that the conclusions can have no definite meaning if the original concepts have none.

23. There is another type of behaviour relationship which can be used in both standard and change contexts, and which can be derived from the first section of the operating account. I refer to the relationship between stocks and gross or net outputs. In particular, changes in stocks of finished goods should be related to changes in sales of finished goods. There is also some evidence for thinking that a standard relationship between total stocks and gross output may be log-normal. Thus, Whitin[1] has suggested that in some trades there is a proportional behaviour relationship between stocks and the square root of gross output. On a wider national background the relationship of movements in stocks (including work-in-progress) to changes in total demand for goods and services is important, for this relates changes in stocks to changes in the general economic and financial situation. It is interesting to notice that this relationship in real terms does not seem to move up and down in quite the same proportions. In a recent *Bulletin for Industry*[2] the following table was given to show

that changes in the rate at which the physical quantity of stocks (ignoring price changes) has been increased or reduced is frequently an important element in the changes in total demand.

(£m. at 1948 factor cost)

Annual Change	*1950*	*1951*	*1952*	*1953*
In investment in stocks and work-in-progress	−214	+622	−405	+108
In total demand for goods and services*	+321	+779	−352	+618

* Total gross domestic expenditure plus exports of goods and services.

This table was followed by the comments that:

In 1951, for example, stocks were increased by £440m. (at 1948 factor cost), having been reduced by £182m. in the previous year. As is shown

[1] *The Theory of Inventory Management*, by Thomas M. Whitin (Princeton University Press, 1953; London: Oxford University Press, 1953), p. 95.

[2] *Bulletin for Industry No. 73* (1955).

in the table, the consequent swing round in investment in stocks of £622m. was a major factor in the big increase in demand that year (£779m.). In the following year, the fact that stock-building fell back from £440m. to only £35m. caused a decline in investment in stocks of £405m. which, as shown in the table, was rather greater than the fall in total demand in that year. In 1953, investment in stocks increased again and contributed to the recovery in total demand. These changes were much more pronounced in some industries than in others.

From the standpoint of attention to background statistics it is especially interesting to notice that another table was included in the *Bulletin for Industry* which showed that changes in the balance of payments had coincided closely with those in investment in stocks and in total demand. The figures given were as under:

£(m.)

	1950	*1951*	*1952*	*1953*
External current balance (excluding defence aid)	300	−407	138	115

The *Bulletin for Industry* had these comments to make:

When stocks fell in 1950 there was a surplus on the balance of payments; in 1951 when stocks were built up there was a deficit; in 1952 when stock-building declined again there was again a surplus. These changes in the current external balance were of course the result of the whole complex of movements in trade associated with the Korean boom and aftermath. But the changes in investment in stocks, partly induced by the sharp rise and fall in prices were, through their effect on imports, one of the important causes of the change in the external balance.

This suggests a case for steady and consistent behaviour relations between stocks and outputs, both for industries and firms as well as for the economy as a whole. Indeed, as the *Bulletin for Industry* points out:

It is necessary to have early knowledge about all stock trends if action is to be taken by the government and by business itself to anticipate, or mitigate, excessive stock movements and so avoid disturbances to the balance of the economy both internally and externally. . . . Industry and commerce, as well as the government, stand to profit from fuller current intelligence.

For the individual firm, changes in stocks of finished goods should be smartly noted, and stocks of raw materials and inventories of work-in-progress, together should be standard with gross outputs, unless there is some valid cause for stock speculation.

24. In *Accounting Dynamics—II*, I suggested the following form as appropriate for the second section of the operating account

	Period 1	Period 2	Change		Period 1	Period 2	Change
8. OPERATIVE AND ANCILLARY LABOUR (wages, salaries and social insurance contributions), adjusted for change in the labour content of work-in-progress ...	x	x	x	7. THE ACCOUNTING MEASUREMENT OF NET OUTPUT or value added ...	x	x	x
9. SELLING AND DISTRIBUTION—Wages, salaries, and social insurance contributions (varying with output)	x	x	x				
	x	x	x				
10. VARIABLE MARGIN ...	x	x	x				
	x	x	x		x	x	x

25. When we come to interpret the second section of the operating account a special significance can be given to the development of a series of relationships, both standard and change, between various categories of direct labour and gross and net outputs. Past behaviour experience and the nature of operating activities should decide the significant categories. Wages, salaries and social insurance contributions spent on the organization of selling and distribution may be expected to follow the same pattern as goods and services purchased in connection with the sale and distribution of products. Accordingly, we should look for a relation between a change in wages, salaries and social insurance contributions expended on the sale and distribution of the product and a change in the sales of the product itself, although here

again this relation may neither necessarily nor immediately appear between the recorded changes of the same time period.

If the relation between changes in goods and services consumed to changes in gross output is constant, then the relation between net output and direct labour becomes very significant. A positive change in direct and ancillary labour consumed may be accompanied by either a positive increasing or decreasing change in outputs, and and the essential task is to judge whether such a change in outputs has compensated for the related change in input.

Deviations from standard relationships (the normal expectations) can be looked upon as measures to validate past management judgements and at the same time as aids to management judgements in the future. Nevertheless, there are reservations about the recognition of the relationship between labour and net output as a production function. As we know, any change in the capital input when it occurs, which is accounted for by a betterment in operating asset usage or technological improvement, will change this function. Moreover, as most of us are aware, the quality of entrepreneurial effort can be a decided variable despite the fixed expense carry in a later part of the operating account. Nevertheless, if we temporarily set aside these objections and ignore them as cutting across the short period, we can see how the marginal product of direct and ancillary labour varies as its input changes, and this is a valuable pointer to a state and scale of activity generating increasing, constant, or decreasing returns.

26. The relation between labour and output has proved its usefulness in one set of circumstances known to me. In this case the monthly change relationship revealed a sharp unexplained deviation from the standard relationship. In due course the management of the firm discovered that the labour content of a new but similar product had been overlooked. Work on this product was not completed because of an unusual machine breakdown and, as it so happened, was unaccounted for in work-in-progress. This at once drew attention to an inadequacy in the work-in-progress valuation control.

27. In *Accounting Dynamics—III*, I have suggested the following form for the third section of the operating account:

		Period 1	Period 2	Change		Period 1	Period 2	Change
12. PURCHASES of goods and services related to operating facilities and *not* immediately varying with output		x	x	x	11. VARIABLE MARGIN ...	x	x	x
13. LABOUR—Wages, salaries, remuneration and social insurance contributions allocated to—								
i. Standing overheads		x	x	x				
ii. Administration and management ...		x	x	x				
14. CAPITAL:								
i. Rents (imputed or actual) ...	x							
ii. Depreciation of operating assets	x	x	x	x				
Total operating overheads		x	x	x				
15. OPERATING INCOME ...		x	x	x				
		x	x	x		x	x	x

28. Purchases of goods and services related to operating facilities not immediately varying with output contain a number of sub-categories which I have detailed as bank charges, cleaning, insurances, lighting and heating, machine rents, minimum royalties, postages, telephones, telegrams, printing and stationery, professional charges, rates, repairs and maintenance of buildings, repairs and maintenance of plant, machinery, and equipment, servicing of transport equipment, trade subscriptions, travelling and entertaining, and water rates. The labour input for standing overheads will be made up from such items as repairs and maintenance of buildings, repairs and maintenance of plant and machinery, and servicing of transport equipment. There is a valuation problem in regard to the capital input item for

depreciation of operating assets which I do not wish to pursue here, except to say that in this context I think of it as measured in terms of end-period prices.

29. Fixed expenses are closely related to the variable resources with which they are combined. It is important to achieve a proper balance between fixed expenses and variable resources. I have suggested that there are at least six standard relationships which bear upon this point. I give them again.

i. Operating overheads, and the total consumption of goods and services varying with output.
ii. Operating overheads, and the variable labour input.
iii. Operating overheads, and the total variable inputs.
iv. Operating overheads, and net output.
v. Operating overheads, and the variable margin; and
vi. Operating overheads, and gross output.

The change relationships should be associated with these standard relationships. Of the foregoing relationships I regard that which relates operating overheads to net output as the most important because, by means of it, it is possible to decide whether the resources of an enterprise are being employed at a level consistent with the fixed costs involved. In a free enterprise economy the behaviour relation between operating income and operating assets employed is obviously important and in the context of the present discussion I would regard the latter as made up of both fixed and variable assets, although I should regard it as a matter of consequence that the variable working capital assets entering into the calculation were standard in function with their operating counterparts, e.g. output.

30. To summarize, the following are the main operating relationships which, together with their make-up variants and their rates of change, a firm should be interested in:

i. Goods and outside services consumed, and gross output;
ii. Operative and ancillary labour, and net output;
iii. The variable margin, and gross/net outputs; and
iv. Operating overheads, and net output.

I think it is clear from this summary that output estimates are important indicators of accounting results. In the theory of the firm, estimates of product demands are the main decision-making promoters, and in conditions of normal markets for both factors of production and their products, consumer behaviour can be thought of as the ultimate regulator of all accounting forms and relationships.

31. To avoid misconceptions, I am bound once again to draw attention to the difference between the accounting concept and the strict economic view of net output, although it is a simple matter to derive a measurement of the economic aggregate from the pattern of accounts which I have put before you. The accounting concept based on a firm's interests has been made clear from the present discussion so far as we have taken it. The economic concept as used in Census of Production data and input-output analysis requires that all goods and services purchased from outside should enter into the figure of net output. This means that those goods and services purchased from outside which are not treated as varying with output, and therefore included in the third section of the operating account as overheads, must also be dealt with as a deduction from gross output to arrive at, for example, the national income concept of net output or value added. Rents actually paid, included in the capital input, must be similarly deducted from gross output. It is by means of this type of reconciliation that a firm's accounts are brought into line with external background statistics. For example, it would show the contribution to gross domestic product, and explain the relation between a firm's own accounts and Census of Production data. Some of you may know that there is a move in some countries to order national statistics on the basis of the accounting or financial pattern followed in social accounting. This is plainly relevant to the unification of private (especially corporate) and social accounting methods.

32. The design of the operating account we have so far discussed, while it attempts to reconcile accounting and economic ideas, nevertheless leans heavily on the empirical distinction between variable and fixed costs. It has been suggested by some

mathematical statisticians that this distinction, especially when adopted by accountants, is not the ultimate criterion, and that past behaviour may be a better guide to the division between fixed and variable. Mr. Philip Lyle,[1] whose recent death was a cause of sorrow to so many, has reminded us that

> the methods of mathematical statistics are being applied to industrial problems on an ever-increasing scale. The branch applicable to problems of quality control has been adequately dealt with . . . but the methods of regression and correlation and their application to the analysis of production costs and factory operations are not so widely known.

He adds this pertinent observation:

> The usual methods of accountancy enable us to analyse our production costs in many ways, but much useful information is contained in the data which those methods cannot isolate and which can only be extracted by statistical methods.

But he is also careful to make the following reservation:

> The application of such methods must necessarily differ very greatly in different industries, and even among different factories in the same industry.

Nevertheless, I think it is plain, as Mr. Lyle says

> the subdivision of production costs is ultimately of most interest and use to managers and managing directors of industrial undertakings.

33. For the purpose of this discussion I shall aim at over-simplicity and in doing so I ask my statistician friends to bear with me. I shall also adapt many of Mr. Philip Lyle's explanations to my present purpose and make use of one or two of his diagrams. Perhaps I should mention that just before he died, Mr. Lyle asked me to consider his regression analysis of production costs in connection with some work I am currently engaged on, and which has to do with the form and interpretation of accounts. For this reason, and because I am not a mathematical statistician, I take

[1] *Regression Analysis of Production Costs and Factory Operations*, by P. Lyle (London: Oliver and Boyd, 1946), pp. v, vi, 1–5, 183, 184.

the following passages, which constitute the greater part of the introduction, from his book on the *Regression Analysis of Production Costs and Factory Operations*[1] together with the figures to which he refers. I do not think they can be bettered.

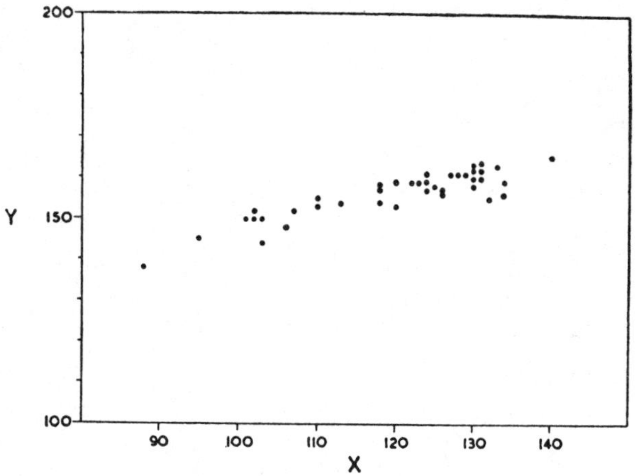

Fig. 1

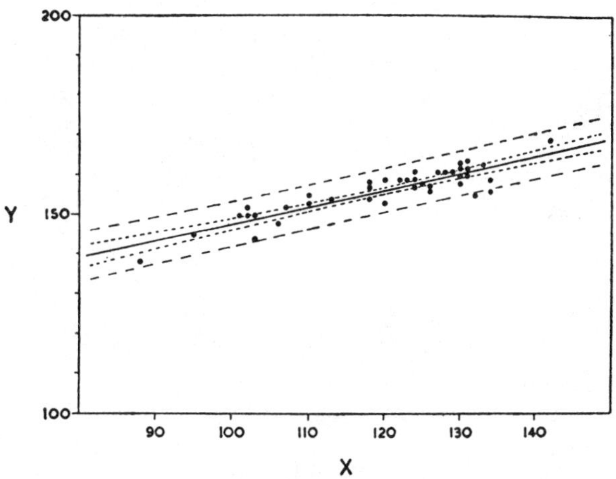

Fig. 1*a*

Fig. 1 is a chart showing the production costs in a factory. The scale on the left-hand side of the chart represents costs in £ per week, the

[1] The reader who wishes to know more about these ideas is specially referred to this work. I am greatly indebted to the executors of the late Philip Lyle and to the publishers for permission to include these extracts.

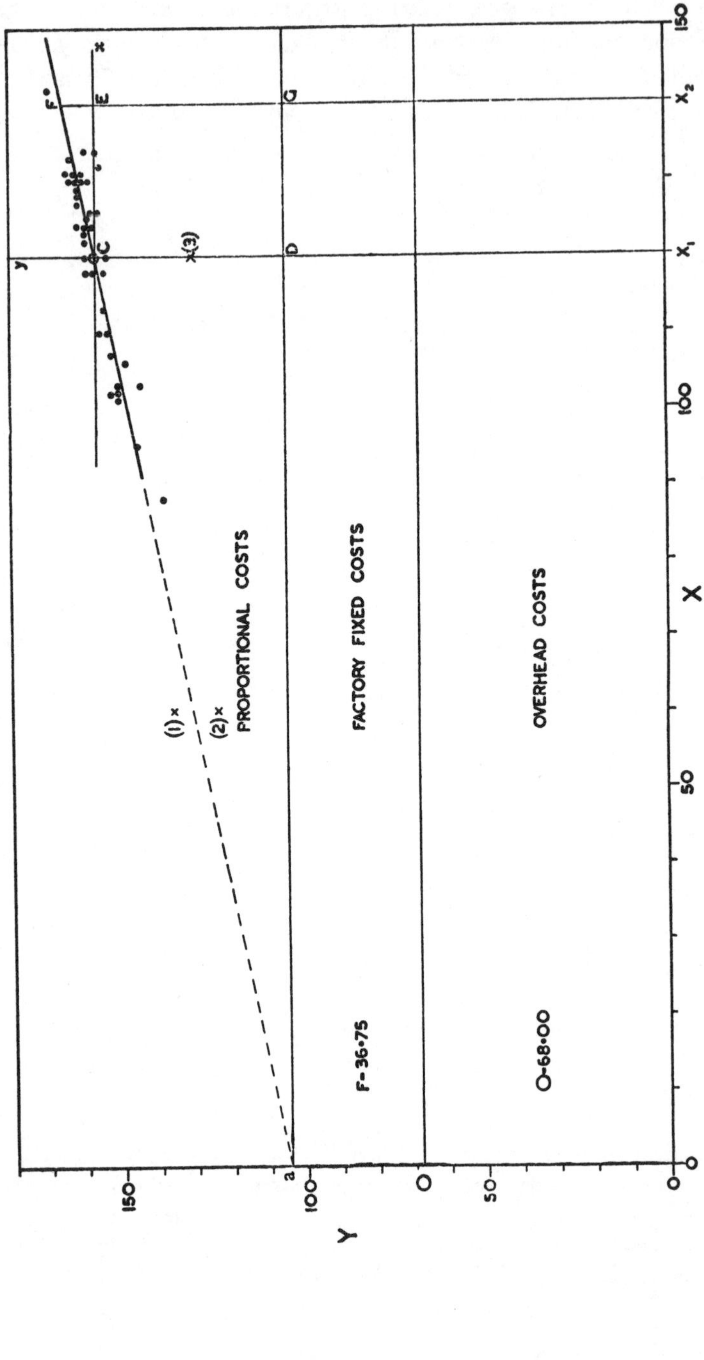
PROPORTIONAL COSTS
FACTORY FIXED COSTS
OVERHEAD COSTS
F-36·75
O-68·00
(1)×
(2)×
×(3)
C
D
E
F
G
a
x
y
X
Y
X_1
X_2
0
50
100
150

Fig. 2

scale at the bottom of the chart being weekly output in tons before packing, the packing, warehousing and delivery costs being dealt with separately. This type of chart is called a 'scatter-diagram' and each point represents the result of one week and shows the total costs in £ corresponding to the particular output in tons for that week. The chart shows the results of forty consecutive weeks.

An inspection of the scatter of the points shows that the general trend is in a straight line sloping upwards to the right, so that higher outputs tend to be associated with higher total costs as we should expect. Now if the output was identical in several weeks we should not expect the costs to come to exactly the same figure each time, for we know that the costs are affected by many other factors as well as output. It is not surprising therefore to find that the points do not lie exactly on a straight line but exhibit a certain amount of scatter. If we take a piece of thread and stretch it across the chart we can, with a little manipulation, place it so that it appears to represent the general trend of the costs with varying output. . . . Mathematicians have . . . provided us with a method of 'fitting' such a line to the points, taking into account all the pairs of values of the two variates (in the present case costs and 'output'), which is sometimes called the 'line of best fit' but more usually the regression line, and the equation representing this line is called the regression equation.

If the total costs were dependent only on output and there were no other factors present in the factory processes or costing system which would in any way affect the costs, then every point would be found to lie exactly on the regression line . . . and we would say that the 'correlation' was perfect. In practice very many causes, most of them small in themselves, have an effect on the costs in any particular week, for instance mistakes, breakdowns, abnormal waste, errors of weighing and measurement, errors in stock-taking, errors in costing, variations in quality of raw materials, etc., etc., some acting in one direction, some in the other, the combined effect of which we call chance. The result of these 'chance' variations is that the individual points do not all lie on a continuous straight line or curve but produce the scatter diagram. . . . It is possible to test whether these variations are or are not great enough to render the regression line unacceptable as a reliable estimate of the trend of costs with output. If the scatter is very great or the trend appears to be curvilinear instead of rectilinear, the data need further consideration before any analysis is attempted. . . . If the points all lie very close to a straight line, we say that the 'correlation' is high.

Assuming we are dealing with the type of case shown in Fig. 1 where there is no apparent curvilinearity, it is obvious that the costs tend on an average to increase in proportion to output, but not in *direct* proportion. The points in Fig. 2 are identical with those in Fig. 1, but the scale of the diagram has been reduced so as to include an output of zero and the regression line has been added. . . . If we extend the regression line to the left, beyond the range covering the points, we find that it cuts the cost axis (where output=0) at the point £*a* and not at zero. . . .

If we draw a horizontal line through *a*, that portion of the costs which lies above it is seen to be directly proportional to the output, becoming zero when the output is zero, all the portion below the line being always constant and equal to £*a*. It appears that £*a* represents fixed costs which are incurred weekly whatever the output may be. Now we know our ordinary 'overhead' costs as determined by our accountants—yearly or half-yearly—and can spread these over the weeks. Call them £O per week. We mark off O on the costs axis and draw a horizontal line through O as in Fig. 2. O will always be less than *a* and the difference represents fixed costs which are not included in 'overheads' and which we will call 'factory fixed costs'.

34. So much for the theory of the matter. Mr. Lyle goes on to explain how what he calls factory fixed costs arise, and one of his points is of particular interest to us here. Thus,

if we halve the output we do not halve the labour bill for obvious reasons, so we see that of the total factory costs—apart from overheads—a portion have the nature of overheads and are independent of the output. . . . The total fixed costs (£*a*) are thus seen to consist of overheads (£O) and factory fixed costs (£F), as shown in Fig. 2.

The importance of this in relation to marginal cost cannot be denied, and so says Mr. Lyle:

As the points in Fig. 2 lie above a straight line—not a curve—the proportional costs, which become zero when the output is zero, divided by the corresponding output will always give the same figure at all outputs and this figure is the 'marginal cost', i.e. the net cost of increasing the output by one unit.

As most of us know, there are elements of over-simplicity about all this as so far stated, but those who are interested will find the implications fully discussed in Mr. Lyle's book. For the moment

I am only concerned with the method of regression analysis as applied to a formal operating account, and I am thinking in terms of a possible regression derived from two variates—total costs (i.e. labour *plus* operating overheads) and net output or value added—as they appear in a series of comparable accounts. I think this will involve some re-ordering of the operating account as I have stated it so far, if we are to arrive at a fixed labour determinant. Providing that we can work on the assumption that the aggregate consumption cost of goods purchased is in some reasonably constant relationship with gross output, and providing we are prepared to regard goods and outside services purchased in connection with the sale and distribution of finished goods as virtually a set off against gross output, then the direct consumption cost of outside services (section 1 of operating account) should be classified with labour (section 2 of the operating account) for the purposes of deciding the possibility of a total costs/net output regression. It will be immediately apparent that for this exercise the accounting statement of net output is revised. If an experienced fixed part of labour is so determined by means of regression analysis in the way we conjecture, then it will need to be transferred down to the third section of the operating account in order that an experienced variable margin may be measured, and with it reliable calculations of marginal costs and marginal revenues as well as their changes. The management consequences of this manœuvre are obvious.

35. There are other behaviour relationships, as I have hinted, which can be derived from appropriation and capital change accounts, as well as operating accounts. Moreover, as I have noted, the balance sheet is not without its part in the scheme of effective resource user. A strong balance sheet is a good background promoter of expansion, and the development of new projects. Even if liquidity status is below preference a strong net asset position is a good fortification for borrowing. In the capital change account we should expect outlays on new real investment to be formally related with later changes in net output. Again, it is by means of this account that we should discover the effectiveness with which a management has deployed unutilized or unabsorbed

resources. A more precise analysis of all this must await a later occasion. In the meantime, however, I cannot forbear to quote from some concluding remarks contained in a report of the Cowles Commission for Research in Economics.[1]

There is ample precedent, in the natural and social sciences alike, for the belief that a free rein to intellectual curiosity may open up the pathways to useful and applicable knowledge more readily than a carefully charted plan of approach. In the selection of problems for investigation and of methods of study, the criterion of intellectual stimulation to open minds takes at least an equal place with any other relevant criteria.

[1] Cowles Commission for Research in Economics, *Report for Period 1 July, 1952 to 30 June, 1954* (University of Chicago, 1954), p. 24.

8

CAPITAL CHANGES

A research lecture delivered at Incorporated Accountants Hall, London, on 14th June, 1956

1. In *Accounting Dynamics—I*, I began the analysis of a formal capital change account following on my previous treatment of this account in *The Formal Principles of Public Company Accounting*, where for utilitarian reasons I styled it a 'Sources, Earmarkings and Utilization of Funds' statement. To set up one main account, as I did there, may give too broad a view of capital changes. Accordingly, I began a breakdown into certain well-defined sectional accounts.

2. In *Accounting Dynamics—I*, I gave the first of these sectional accounts. I limited it to the *real* aggregates of capital change, and I called it saving and asset formation. I dealt with its operating implications, and for that reason passed on to a formal analysis of the operating account. For the sake of completeness I again illustrate the sectional capital change account for saving and asset formation.

CAPITAL CHANGE ACCOUNTS

(i) Saving and Asset Formation.

1. NET EXPENDITURE on:			1. RETAINED INCOME of the accounting period ...	x	
i. Tangible fixed assets ...	x		2. EARMARKED INCOME of the accounting period (redemptions and reserves)	x	
ii. Intangible fixed assets	x			—	x
	—	x	3. PROVISION FOR DEPRECIATION		
2. INCREASE (or decrease negative) in deferred expenditure		x	i. Cost allocation ...	x	
3. INCREASE (or decrease negative) in total inventories ...		x	ii. Price change adjustment (increase positive, or decrease negative) ...	x	
		—		—	x
		x	4. INVENTORY price change adjustment (increase positive, or decrease negative) ...		x
					—
					x
4. BALANCE—Excess saving ...		x	5. BALANCE—Excess asset formation		x
		—			—
		x			x
		═			═

I should perhaps add that the link between the item for operating profit in the operating account and the item for retained income of the accounting period in the present account, is constituted by financial incomings (e.g. income from investments) and financial outgoings (e.g. debenture interest) and the general run of appropriation account items, of which perhaps the most important are direct income taxation and dividend distributions. These were set out in the *Formal Principles of Public Company Accounting*, but whereas there we were concerned with a statutory fit, that is not here our purpose, and as a consequence some items such as transactions of a sort not usually undertaken will show elsewhere.

3. The essential object of these sectional capital change accounts is to bring about a combination of facts and theory, and as a consequence, I should wish to separate off valuation adjustments brought about by changes in the value of money. Quite properly, however, two of these adjustments, the price change adjustment for depreciation and the inventory price change adjustment, have already featured in the sectional account for saving and asset formation in order that it can be expressed in *real* terms, and because both of these adjustments qualify real asset formation. This leaves us with those adjustments which on any strict basis of measurement at the accounting date affect the balance sheet statement of real assets brought in at the beginning of an accounting period. In those cases where such adjustments are taken into account the *capital* adjustment will be credited and the *asset* adjustment debited.[1] It will be seen that these adjustments are counterbalancing and involve no residual balance. Accordingly, there is little point in treating them in a separate account and ordinarily a separate balance sheet notation should suffice. Nevertheless, we should learn from the size of these counterbalancing adjustments whether the price change in real asset values has either influenced or kept in step with a related variation in short-term or current financial claims, and we should investigate the manner in which this variation has been financed. We should also determine whether or not this related variation is standard having regard to past showings in similar circumstances. Experience

[1] Increases—positive, decreases—negative.

should tell us the mathematical nature of this relationship, if such there be.

4. As we have agreed to by-pass valuation adjustments, the next sectional capital change account which I think follows in logical sequence, is that for gains and losses. I give an outline illustration of its form.

(ii) Gains and Losses.

1. CAPITAL LOSSES (itemized, e.g. unforeseen obsolescence) ...	x	1. CAPITAL GAINS (itemized, e.g. in the limited context of private enterprise—a profit on realization of fixed assets or realized goodwill formerly unaccounted for. In the wider context of social accounting—a valuation of wealth within the ownership of the entity, newly discovered in the current accounting period)	x
2. INTERMEDIATE LOSSES derived from transactions of a sort not usually undertaken ...	x	2. INTERMEDIATE GAINS derived from transactions of a sort not usually undertaken ...	x
3. BAD DEBTS	x	3. ADJUSTMENTS to past income measures	x
4. ADJUSTMENTS to past income measures	x		
	x		x
5. BALANCE—RESIDUARY GAIN ...	x	4. BALANCE—RESIDUARY LOSS	x
	x		x

5. The construction of this sectional capital change account for gains and losses really derives from the notion of *income* as a flow. In *Accounting Dynamics—I*, I referred to income as a flow and capital as a stock, and I said it follows from this that capital changes are represented by variations in stocks of possessions and financial claims, while income changes are brought about by alterations in flow transactions. Since the economic process is continuous through time, flow transactions go on more or less continuously. Thus, *income* should not be regarded as a valuation concept. Capital gains and losses, whether realized or unrealized, fall outside the measurement of income because they form no part of an intentionally designed operating flow. They are not repetitive or continuous transactions. In the present account we should normally confine ourselves to realized gains or losses because

unrealized gains or losses are usually covered by valuation adjustments.

6. The main feature which I associate with either a capital loss or a capital gain is its irregularity. It is usually unpremeditated unless foreseeable circumstances change. Thus, the loss or gain should be unforeseen and unexpected, uncertain and reasonably fortuitous. For example, it is not a normal characteristic of a *fixed* asset to its owner that it should have been acquired for re-sale involving either loss or gain. In general terms a capital loss brings about a set back, and a capital gain a set forward in recorded wealth ownership. Four examples have been cited in the sectional account. Unforeseen obsolescence has been itemized as a capital loss precisely because it is unforeseen. In the limited context of private enterprise a profit on realization of fixed assets, and an amount of realized goodwill formerly unaccounted for, are treated as capital gains. In the wider context of social or national accounting a valuation of newly discovered wealth becomes a capital gain. This last example clearly illustrates a 'jump' forward in recorded national wealth.

7. The sectional capital change account for losses and gains attempts the sorting out of quasi-exceptional transactions from regular flow transactions. As a consequence, it would seem that intermediate gains and losses should be dealt with in this account, although some people will no doubt want to argue that such losses and gains are not directly classifiable either as capital or income. Nevertheless, in setting up this account I follow a legal description contained in The Companies Act, 1948, and so define intermediate gains and losses as derivatives from transactions of a sort not usually undertaken. You will remember that the Eighth Schedule (14) requires the disclosure of any material respects in which any items shown in the profit and loss account are affected by transactions of a sort not usually undertaken by the company or otherwise by circumstances of an exceptional or non-recurrent nature. The practice of accounting thereby gets over the difficulty of economic definition by relying upon a disclosure philosophy. In the descriptive definition used here, intermediate gains and losses are not continuous, and they do not form part of an intentionally

designed operating flow. Despite the naming of them as *intermediate*, I therefore lean to their inclusion on that side of the fence which contains capital changes. In this way measurements of operating income and its make-up variants are kept precise and distinct.

8. In *Accounting Dynamics—IV*, I dealt with the theoretical treatment of bad debts and explained why I regarded this item as a capital loss. You will remember the argument. 'Sales converted into debtors become financial claims due to the enterprise. As such they are part of its capital structure. If they fail to be liquidated into cash they become capital losses chargeable as such in the capital change account.'

9. The next item which calls for some brief comments in this sectional capital change account for gains and losses is the adjustment to past income measures. For obvious reasons it is an item which can appear on either side of the account. Corrections to past income measurements subsequently discovered, a not unfamiliar experience even when well regulated practices of accounting prevail, should not be allowed either to disturb or distort the clarity of the measurement of current income and its appropriation. Accordingly, I think it should be brought into the present account, and I would require that it *was* so brought in because in the nature of things this adjustment was never anticipated or expected in the current accounting period. This puts it on a par with capital and intermediate gains and losses.

10. The balance on the account now under discussion may be said to represent, in general terms, a residual gain or loss of an irregular or unpremeditated nature. Irregularity and unpremeditatedness when considered in the context of the items appearing in this sectional account do not make for very satisfactory functional relationships between these and other types of accounting aggregates, either bilateral or dynamic, except perhaps in the special case of bad debts which is presumably relateable to balance sheet aggregates for debtors and credit experience over time. But this is not to say that the gains and losses we are dealing with are irrelevant to operating management. For example, in *Accounting Dynamics—IV*, I made the point that 'capital losses are

just as much a matter for management concern as operating expenses, and there are many instances of strictly theoretical capital losses necessarily incurred for trading purposes which are thereby properly allowable as charges against profits for taxation purposes.' Nevertheless, when all is said and done on the score of irregularity and unforeseenness, it might well transpire that over time the gains and losses we are considering may reveal, what I should like to call, some fortuitous regularity or relationship with some other accounting aggregates. It is possible to see that this might happen in the case of obsolescence. Thus, obsolescence debits might conceivably show a functional relationship with balance sheet levels of classified fixed assets over time, and whether or not this arose from a debatable gross or net[1] level of fixed asset aggregates at current prices, as one term in the relationship, it is possible to proceed with an argument that, in fact, such obsolescence has become consequentially foreseeable, and subsequently, therefore, should be taken account of in operating measurements of depreciation. This would take it off the sectional capital change account for gains and losses, a departure which should commend itself to management policy. If a similar approach could be applied to other capital gains and losses and indeed, as well to intermediate gains and losses, it might be taken to imply that operating predictions were becoming more reliable and all-inclusive. This would mean such improved operating predictions that in the last analysis the sectional capital change account for gains and losses would be restricted to the loss and gain results of exogenous, unusual or involuntary happenings. This is seemingly but a way of perfection in both design and forecast to be strived after, but it is also possible to see in all this that it could make for a very illuminating sectional capital change account, bumped up perhaps at intervals by currently unexpected happenings and slowed down again no doubt as management's knowledge of the one-time unexpected becomes regardable as relatively normal and foreseeable.

11. The next and third sectional account which I wish to consider is that for long-term financial changes, and I suggest that it be set up in the following form.

[1] i.e. less accumulated provisions for depreciation.

(iii) Long Term Financial Changes.

1. SECURITY INVESTMENTS (New—positive, realized—negative)	x	1. CAPITAL (New—positive, repaid—negative) ...	x
2. LONG-TERM LENDING (New—positive, repaid—negative)	x	2. LONG-TERM BORROWING (New—positive, repaid—negative)	x
	x		x
3. BALANCE—Funds introduced	x	3. BALANCE—Funds invested	x
	x		x

12. This sectional account for long-term financial changes can be framed, and the items in it sub-classified, to give both a detailed disposition of invested funds and the sources of introduced funds. Nevertheless, the real significance of the account lies in its balances and the manner in which they are relatable to other aggregates. This will come up for discussion on the summary account of capital change, but in general it can be said that for a long-term sectional account of this nature one would expect some kind of relationship with either fixed asset formation or unutilized saving.

13. The fourth sectional account is devoted to working capital changes, and is set up in the following form.

(iv) Working Capital Changes.

1. CHANGES IN CURRENT ASSET CLAIMS: (Increases—positive, decreases—negative)			1. CHANGES IN CURRENT LIABILITY CLAIMS: (Increases — positive, decreases—negative)		
i. Short-term lending ...	x		i. Short term borrowing	x	
ii. Customers' credit ...	x		ii. Suppliers' credit ...	x	
iii. Unexpired claims ...	x		iii. Accruals	x	
		x	iv. Dividend and interest claims	x	
2. SHORT-TERM MARKETABLE SECURITY INVESTMENTS: (Increases—positive, decreases—negative) ...		x	v. Current tax liabilities	x	
					x
3. INCREASE IN MONETARY BALANCES		x	2. DECREASE IN MONETARY BALANCES		x
		x			x
4. BALANCE—Decrease in Working Capital		x	3. BALANCE—Increase in Working Capital		x
		x			x

14. Sectional account (iv) like sectional account (iii) is concerned with changes in financial claims, the one short-term and the other long-term. Since in this treatment of capital changes an

increase or decrease in inventories has been dealt with as a part of *real* asset formation in sectional account (i), working capital (and its changes—sectional account (iv)) is limited to the restlessness of short-term financial claims. To a large extent both sectional accounts (iii) and (iv) reveal the financial effects of those deeper realities represented by changes in asset formation and changes in outputs. As we have already suggested of the balances in sectional account (iii) one would expect to find some kind of inner bilateral relationship with either asset-formation or saving, while in the case of sectional account (iv) and its balances one would look for a similar type of relationship with net outputs, that is, the changing magnitudes of value added. Nevertheless, the funds introduced at (iii) may in fact have financed a necessary expansion at (iv) represented by an increase in working capital brought about by reason of expanding net outputs. Contrawise a contrived decrease at (iv) regarded as persistent because of contracting net outputs, may have occasioned a long-term investment of funds at (iii), but these are questions of bilateral relationship which the summary account of capital change should reveal in specific cases.

15. If we look carefully at the items included in the sectional account for working capital changes we shall probably feel that short-term borrowing and lending, and short-term marketable security investments should be generally regarded as falling within the same category as monetary balances. Accruals and unexpired claims are items relevant to periodicity and we should not expect them to exert much influence on working capital changes if the accounting treatment was consistent and normal, and no great change had been experienced to a scale of activity making for increased overheads. Changes in dividend and interest claims by themselves, and if reasonably proportional to changes in income, do not call for much comment in this context. Moreover, a change in unpaid tax liabilities can hardly be thought of as a causative influence on a real working capital change in any operating sense. A net change in debtors and creditors, or as here described, customers' and suppliers' credits, should be a straightforward function (though possibly log-normal) of changes in net output, always provided that regularity of credit conduct can be assumed.

We should expect a function of this order because net output, apart from changes in inventories, is itself dependent upon sales and purchases of goods and services. Reasonable monetary balances facilitate an experienced and easy flow of receipts and payments. If then we limit our working capital change to a derivative of changes in debtors and creditors and monetary balances, and provided there is no marked variation in the behaviour of these items which would alter their relative weights, then there is a hard core of probability that our limited working capital change will turn out to be functionally related to changes in net output.

16. There is a point of view which asserts that working capital changes vary with *real asset formation* or a fixed asset restriction within real asset formation, and sometimes rather more obscurely that working capital as deduced from a balance sheet varies with its counterpart aggregate for fixed assets; and indeed these relationships whether regarded as bilateral or dynamic may have some indirect validity. Nevertheless, I think them circuitous because working capital would seem to be primarily dependent upon the size of net output or production value, and that is what one would expect. Admittedly it is an expanding net output which may induce asset formation as well as increased working capital, but I should prefer to regard the latter as more directly relatable to net output and less directly, or only consequentially, to asset formation.

17. The fifth sectional capital change account which I should wish to set up is described in terms of tax adjustments and changes in provisions and deferred liabilities. I illustrate it in the following form.

(v) Tax adjustments and changes in Provisions and Deferred Liabilities.

1. TAX ADJUSTMENTS on Capital and Intermediate Gains and Losses (where relevant)	x	1. CHANGES IN PROVISIONS (Increases—positive, decreases—negative) ...	x
2. ADJUSTMENTS to past taxation transfers	x	2. CHANGES IN DEFERRED LIABILITIES: (Increases—positive, decreases—negative) ...	x
	x		x
3. BALANCE—Residuary credit	x	3. BALANCE—Residuary debit	x
	x		x

18. It will be seen that sectional account (v) picks up the tax adjustments which may consequentially follow the inclusion within capital changes of such items as appear in sectional account (ii) for gains and losses. It by no means follows that the inclusion of an item in sectional account (ii) will necessarily involve a tax adjustment. A number of items brought under capital gains and losses will be clear of United Kingdom taxation, but intermediate gains and losses, and adjustments to past income measures may very well involve tax adjustments, and it would seem that these are best dealt with in this miscellaneous sectional account (v). Changes in provisions and changes in deferred liabilities may give rise to relatively temporary capital credits or debits, taken up or utilized in the manner our summary account will shortly reveal. As a consequence they have been given their place here. Again, and as one might expect, the probable irregularity of the aggregates in this sectional account (v) will hardly make them relatable to other aggregates appearing elsewhere in the structure of accounts, except in a few rather obvious bilateral cases[1] which of themselves cannot be regarded as fundamental. Nevertheless, it might be interesting to see from past capital change data how far temporary residual credits of the kind thrown up in sectional account (v) have been relied upon to finance partial asset formations or expansions in working capital, and equally when they caught up with themselves in the form of residual debits to represent a piece of delayed financing out of normal incoming capital resources.

19. As a commentary on the preceding paragraph, I should like to mention that I know of a factual inquiry into the finance of companies as limited to two specific trades covering the years 1947–51, which among its conclusions contained a statement to the effect that large investments in stocks had been financed out of future tax reserves and a partial running down of liquid balances. The inquiry pointed out the dangers involved when operating assets were financed by *increases* in future tax reserves, and drew attention to the consequential inadequacy of the liquid assets to cover future tax payments if a period of falling prices should follow.

[1] e.g. changes in operating incomes and changes in deferred taxation liabilities.

Such a warning is equally applicable to a long-term financial utilization of *increases* in other deferred liabilities and *increases* in provisions. It will be apparent from this latter comment that I regard a future tax reserve as a deferred liability.

20. The present analysis of capital changes can now be presented in the following summary form.

(vi) Summary Account of Capital Changes.

	Intended or expected standards of change.	Actual changes.	Differences.		Intended or expected standards of change.	Actual changes.	Differences.
i. Excess asset formation	x	x	x	i. Excess saving (and sometimes disinvestment)	x	x	x
ii. Residuary loss ...	x	x	x	ii. Residuary gain ...	x	x	x
iii. Funds invested (or possibly in special cases, withdrawn or transferred)	x	x	x	iii. Funds introduced ...	x	x	x
iv. Increase in working capital	x	x	x	iv. Decrease in working capital	x	x	x
v. Residuary debit ...	x	x	x	v. Temporary residuary credit	x	x	x
	x	x	x		x	x	x
Asset valuation adjustment	–	x	–	Capital valuation adjustment	–	x	–
	x	x	x		x	x	x

21. At paragraph 3, we decided that there was little or no point in having a separate sectional account for valuation adjustments. It will be remembered that the adjustments in question were those which on a strict basis of measurement at the accounting date specially affected the balance sheet statement of real assets brought in at the beginning of an accounting period, and indeed, theoretically, we should not exclude real asset formation at any time within the interval of the period itself if any marked valuation change has occurred which has not already been covered in sectional account (i). It was decided not to have a separate sectional account, because any debit for asset valuation adjustment would have a corresponding credit for the capital valuation adjustment. The adjustments

were counterbalancing and so no residual balance was involved. Nevertheless, in the summary account now put forward it is desirable to include these valuation adjustments in order that we end up with a complete statement of capital changes for whatever period of account may be relevant. A valuation adjustment arising from the presence of *real* operating assets will need to be included in any calculation of operating capital employed if the measurement of the latter concept is to establish its functional relationship with a measurement of operating income. In other words, if effective management is assumed, a valuation adjustment of this order should be relatable to some change in operating income, either bilaterally or in a subsequent period of account.

22. It will be noticed that in the summary account there are separate headings for intended or expected standards of change, actual changes, and consequential differences. If the expected standards of change were so contrived as to fit in with the operating account and balance sheet functional patterns of an intended best use of resources, these differences should indicate the skew effects on the wealth structure of an entity as a consequence of its inability to keep to its own behaviour standards.

23. Similar headings to those included in the summary account of capital changes could be extended to the sectional accounts themselves. In sectional account (i) for example, intended saving could be contrasted with realized saving; or again, intended investment (asset formation) with realized investment. This type of contrast would then promote some such questions as how far did actual results fall short of the entrepreneur's intentions for proper reasons retrospectively discerned, or how far did they just come upon him in random fashion, and why?

24. It will be noticed that the residual aggregate debits and credits in the summary account are largely alternative. They are not usually both present at the same time. Thus, it is either excess asset formation or excess saving, either residuary loss or residuary gain and so on. As a consequence, the main interpretation of capital change rests on the bilateral relationships between five net aggregates, and for those who like to see these things in simple narrative form we can set up the following table

with the residuary aggregates in either positive or negative terms as their measurements require. These positives and negatives will always counterbalance to give a zero total. Thus, the negatives account for the positives.

CAPITAL CHANGE:

i. Excess asset formation (+) or excess saving (and sometimes *disinvestment* (−)	x
ii. Residuary loss (+) or residuary gain (−)	x
iii. Net funds invested (+) or net funds introduced (−)	x
iv. Increase (+) or decrease (−) in working capital	x
v. Miscellaneous residuary debit (+) or temporary residuary credit (−)	x
	zero

25. As we have seen, the bilateral functions of capital change are very largely disclosed in the summary account. The dynamic functions, as one would expect, mainly emanate from sectional account (i). Both sets of functions should be read and interpreted together. Material for the time-shape of real investment is plainly at hand if an accounting series has been maintained on the lines set out both here and in *Accounting Dynamics*. It may be remembered that Professor J. R. Hicks has much to say on the subject of induced investment in his book on the Trade Cycle.[1] The following situation which he describes should be evidentially confirmed over time from our formal structures of accounts. Thus, 'suppose that there is an increase in output (we need not inquire for what reason), and that the increase is expected to be permanent—the new level is to be maintained indefinitely. For the production of the new output the existing capital stock will no longer be appropriate. In the *short period*, the enlarged output can be produced, but only by using the capital equipment at more than its optimum intensity, and therefore (in all probability) increasing its effective rate of depreciation; this provides a motive for increasing the stock of equipment. Thus the increase in output induces investment; investment occurs as part of the process of moving from one equilibrium to the other'.[2]

[1] Oxford, Clarendon Press, 1950.

[2] *Ibid.*, p. 40.

26. In this discussion on the dynamic properties of capital change we are, of course, neglecting the associated effects of changes in operating inputs other than capital, in particular labour in its several forms, on changes in output. Again, it seems clear that both sets of functions should be read and interpreted together, although the operating functions will probably be more bilateral than dynamic. Professor Hicks in his summing up on induced investment in fact indicates, as it seems to me, the kind of dynamic relationship one should look for when a series of sectional capital change accounts (especially (i) and (iv)) is referred against a series of operating accounts designed in the manner suggested in *Accounting Dynamics*. Therefore, I quote him. 'The characteristic effect on investment of a rise in the demand for output seems to be capable of division into three phases. In the first phase there is a tendency to disinvestment; the additional output is not yet forthcoming, and the additional demand is satisfied (so far as it can be satisfied) out of stocks. Towards the end of this phase the rate of disinvestment diminishes, because the decumulation of stocks is offset by accumulation of working capital. Thus the first phase passes, not sharply but gradually, into the second, in which the main part of the induced investment takes place. This has to include (1) investment in stocks, to make up for the raiding of stocks in the first phase; (2) investment in fixed capital, needed to adjust equipment to the production of the larger output. The positive net investment which is needed in this phase may be very large indeed. Finally, there is a third phase, stretching into the remoter future, which is troubled by oscillations in investment due to the alternate building up and running down of depreciation reserves in the process of replacement. This last is purely a problem of fixed capital; there seems to be nothing corresponding to it on the working capital side.

The characteristic effects of a fall in the demand for output can be classified in a similar way. Here again there is a first phase in which the effect goes in the 'wrong' direction—the fall in demand leads to positive investment in stocks, 'surplus stocks' as they will become. It is followed by a second phase, in which disinvestment occurs; the surplus stocks are gradually disposed of, and fixed equipment is gradually reduced by cessation of replacement. But although the total amount of disinvestment which has to occur in this phase is comparable (for an equal change in demand) to the total amount of investment which has to occur in the corresponding phase of the other movement, it is likely to be much more spread out in time. Because of this spreading out, the third phase (the 'tail') is of negligible importance in this case.'[1]

27. We might perhaps take advantage of our little excursion into trade cycle theory to consider whether finance and accounting has anything to contribute in this field. The borrowing potential of an enterprise is mainly dependent upon its prospective earning capacity, very largely judged from past results, and its asset cover. All accountants will know how difficult it is to borrow on prospective earning capacity unless it is supported by the trend of past earnings, and there is adequate asset cover for the borrowing. Apart from the ability to attract new money capital which has its own limitations, the financial limits on net asset formation in any one accounting period may be thought of in terms of saving plus any unutilized borrowing potential. The complete borrowing potential of an enterprise is apt to be limited in two directions, one by some acceptable proportion of the value of its net assets dependent on their nature, and two, by the present amount of its employed proprietorship capital. Such financial limits may well exercise a check on *real* investment, and have some influence on retarding income generation in the capital goods industries where a downturn is apt to start (demand side). This is quite apart from other and probably more cogent considerations elsewhere such as over-capacity on the supply side.

28. Capital changes invite a number of pertinent questions. For example, we should be concerned to know whether the rate of return on new investment exceeds the market compensation rate. We should want to examine the pattern of changes in *real* operating assets allied to changes in net financial claims with changes in net outputs. Moreover, the measures of such changes per operative employee have their uses. In some cases operating cost reductions should be relatable to increased physical investment. Managements

[1] *Op. cit.*, pp. 51–52.

must recognize the financial implications of capital expenditure. I think it should always promote either justifiable increases in net output or proportionate savings in factor costs and standing charges. Sometimes all three will be present at the same time. The use of capital resources is a matter of consequence to an enterprise, especially, as we have said, the measurement of the expected and realized return on new *real* operating assets plus additional working financial resources as contrasted with the cost of the new money so locked up. In so far as is contrivable the marginal net productivity of capital should not fall below the long-term borrowing rate as well as the marginal productivity of competing investment projects. As a general rule, the return on new investment should stay ahead of the long-term borrowing rate.

29. Capital expenditure on asset formation is a flow through time and for a continuing entity this flow should be maintained whatever the rate of saving, but it is probably true to say that in the long run the rate of flow will be varied according to the rate of saving plus depreciation, notwithstanding borrowing potentials and expectations, except possibly in the case of certain specially fortified or risk impervious entities. Nevertheless, a borrowing potential is important when there is an adequate available supply of funds, and when the cost of borrowing is below expected asset returns, for then a present willingness to engage in asset formation may be temporarily quickened. But there are other implications which affect the rate of flow of capital expenditure. Capital construction can be a drawn-out affair during which costs may change. Again, the availability of materials may alter; unforeseen technical difficulties may arise, and if it is overseas investment which is in point exchange rates may be variable. Some provision may have to be made for a change in the project. Unavoidable capital expenditure may arise which is in the nature of a social cost, and some asset formation with but a small return may be necessary to maintain the earnings of a substantial investment already made. But perhaps we are not so concerned with a rate of flow as with a rate of growth in which case the conclusions to be drawn from a series of capital change accounts over time should have much to offer.

PART TWO

9

THE NATURE AND PURPOSE OF DIRECT TAXATION

A lecture delivered on 20th September, 1953, at a course for Incorporated Accountants at King's and Caius Colleges, Cambridge

1. As is fitting in a course of this kind, we have felt that our main concern was with the machinery and administration of taxation. It is our job to help our clients and the Inland Revenue with proper measurements of income and capital, and to make sure that at those points where we touch the system as professional advisers, we cause it to run smoothly and justly. Nevertheless, we too are taxpayers, for none of us escape the mesh. We *feel* the burden, and when we conjoin these personal feelings with professional experiences gathered from years of watchfulness over other people's affairs, we sometimes find ourselves uneasy at the gathering momentum of direct taxation which time has revealed. It, therefore, becomes us to re-examine some principles in the hope of gaining a better understanding of its purpose.

2. It is but a commonplace to remark on the growth of activity in the public sector of the national economy. The State has brought under its canopy larger and larger commitments necessitating bigger and bigger transfers of income to meet them. The machinery of direct taxation is a complex means of arriving at a simple end: namely the utilization of part of the value added by economic activity in society to the outlay needs of the Central Government or, if you so prefer, a means of assessing and collecting individual and institutional contributions for application to the purposes of common spending and investment. Mrs. Hicks has recently told us that in the early 1870's total taxes amounted to about 8 per cent of the national income; in 1953 they were approximately 40 per cent, and as most of us know 50 per cent of the latest figure of gross fixed asset formation 'is now on public account'.[1]

[1] 'The Budget as an Instrument of Policy, 1837–1953', by Ursula K. Hicks—*The Three Banks Review*, June, 1953, pp. 16–17.

It was not so very long ago that people simply thought taxation should be equal (not that incomes should be equal), and that it should be directed to the maintenance of the revenue, not to the guidance of commerce.[1] We still hear echoes of this point of view.

3. Direct taxation has been with us for some years now, and as we are thinking in terms of principles it is unlikely that anything very new or original will show itself. Nevertheless, it is instructive to go back and look at what earlier writers have had to say on the subject, and to judge their views in relation to the legacies of two major wars and changing social concepts. Most of us will recognize that two wars and uncertainty in regard to future strife have perforce imposed magnitudes of strain which no one could have contemplated in the calmer moments of the past. Perhaps after all, it is not surprising that our present tax structure looks such a patchwork job.

4. Adam Smith, influenced by the social climate of his day, thought of those expenses of the Sovereign, laid out for the general benefit of society, in terms of defence, the dignity of the chief magistrate, justice, roads and communications, education and religious instruction. These expenses are still of paramount importance, but there are interesting comments about education and religious instruction which bear repetition. Thus:

> The expense of the institutions for education and religious instruction is likewise, no doubt, beneficial to the whole society, and may, therefore, without injustice, be defrayed by the general contribution of the whole society. This expense, however, might perhaps with equal propriety, and even with some advantage, be defrayed altogether by those who receive the immediate benefit of such education and instruction, or by the voluntary contribution of those who think they have occasion for either the one or the other.[2]

5. Adam Smith followed his chapter on the expenses of the Sovereign by a discussion on the sources of revenue, and as is well known, he enumerated the following maxims of taxes in general.

[1] Cf. *Political Economy and Laissez Faire*, by J. E. Cairnes, p. 238.

[2] *The Wealth of Nations*, Everyman edition, Vol. 2, p. 298.

i. The subjects of every state ought to contribute towards the support of the government, as nearly as possible, in proportion to their respective abilities; that is, in proportion to the revenue which they respectively enjoy under the protection of the State.

ii. The tax which each individual is bound to pay ought to be certain, and not arbitrary. The time of payment, the manner of payment, the quantity to be paid, ought all to be clear and plain to the contributor, and to every other person. [No doubt this is still a salutory piece of advice to all concerned with the machinery of direct taxation, but I think we should have a little English fun at the odd sound of the following corollary.] Where it is otherwise, every person subject to the tax is put more or less in the power of the tax-gatherer, who can either aggravate the tax upon any obnoxious contributor, or extort, by the terror of such aggravation, some present or perquisite to himself.

iii. Every tax ought to be so levied at the time, or in the manner, in which it is most likely to be convenient for the contributor to pay it.

iv. Every tax ought to be so contrived at as both to take out and keep out of the pockets of the people as little as possible over and above what it brings into the public treasury of the state.[1]

6. In his Newmarch lectures delivered at the end of 1919, Stamp said that: 'Indisputable as these rules may be, they are now inadequate to the practical task of bringing under judgement the many difficult issues that confront us.'[2] Accordingly he set himself the task of examining the situation from the standpoints of the taxpayer, the central government, and economic society at large. He wanted to find a practical compromise which would be best from all three points of view.

7. Elementally, the taxpayer should look at the benefits he receives from State expenditure. The costs that each person causes the State to incur should be refunded, but, of course, there are social expenditures which benefit poorer people who cannot afford to make refunds, and there are expenditures which promote socially desirable benefits, which some people do not want. Thus, at a comparatively late date in our political history, we evolved the

[1] *Op. cit.*, pp. 307–8.
[2] *The Fundamental Principles of Taxation* (Macmillan, 1936), p. 4.

idea that the natural means of handling the situation was to determine ability to contribute according to resource, or command over goods and services.

8. But this expedient has brought its own problem. In his day, John Stuart Mill wanted equality of sacrifice with its universal sanctions of justice and morality, and he thought of it in terms of 'neither more, nor less inconvenience . . . than every other person experiences from his (contribution)'. In our day, we may be left to wonder whether ability to contribute can be made coterminous with equality of sacrifice, for as our President has implied, the expropriation of wealth from the thrifty must be according to real national needs if redistribution is to be justified. Only just lately Dr. Shehab has said:

> The point at which income is divided (for purposes of taxation) into necessary and superfluous must be decided not solely by the individual's needs but by reference also to national needs. An equilibrium must be struck between the two. It is in the light of both that the distribution of the national income between the private and the public sectors of the national economy must be divided by the legislature, if the best results are to be obtained.[1]

9. The trouble with all this is blatantly apparent, and since it is almost impossible to be original when discussing a political topic of this nature, I make no excuse for drawing upon other people's well expressed comments. As accountants we should be very familiar with 'assumptions which are essentially *conventional* in character'. Therefore, to cite Professor Robbins:

> When, for purposes of discussion of . . . the effects of progressive taxation, we assume that the economic subjects are equally capable of deriving satisfaction from equal increments of income, we are certainly not even pretending to be talking about facts. If we were trying to make statements about the facts of the situation, I suspect that most of us would say that people are not equal in this respect, that their capacity differs enormously. But that, of course, would be neither here

[1] *Progressive Taxation*, by F. Shehab. A Study in the Development of the Progressive Principle in the British Income Tax (Oxford, Clarendon Press, 1953).

nor there. For good or for bad, what we are doing in this connection is to make statements about the logical implications of certain conventions which, at bottom, are *political*. It is as though we had said, society will not be just, or it will not run so as to yield good results, unless we act *as if* the citizens were equally capable of satisfactions.[1]

Plainly there is much wisdom here.

10. I suppose that confiscation as a by-product of graduation has always worried politicians with an economic bent, I suspect it is still troubling them, although this time the question is cast in a different role. Again, I fall back on Dr. Shehab for elucidation: 'There is a point beyond which graduation cannot safely be carried as a permanent feature of the tax structure; evasion and disincentive are two far-reaching factors that would preclude its application in an arbitrary or extortionate form.'[2] And so to the reviewer of Dr. Shehab's book in *The Times Literary Supplement* who puts 'the leading question of today—how to maintain the high yields of taxation which the demands of modern social welfare and of defence alike require without at the same time destroying the incentive to effort'.

11. Stamp has said that 'a progressive produce tax existed in Athens six centuries before Christ, and possibly an income tax in Egypt a thousand years earlier, while in this country there was progression in the fourteenth and fifteenth centuries'.[3] Nevertheless, so far as this country is concerned, the application of progression to incomes never became a basic principle of direct taxation until the development of those economic ideas, associated with wants and their satisfaction, which looked at utility in terms of marginal increments. Marshall, you will remember, framed the matter thus—'If we take a man as he is, without allowing time for any change in his character, the marginal utility of a thing to him diminishes steadily with every increase in his supply of it.'[4] 'A greater utility will be required to induce him to buy a thing if he is poor than if he is rich,'[5] and 'the richer a man becomes the less is the marginal utility of money to him'.[6]

[1] *Robertson on Utility and Scope*, by Lionel Robbins, *Economica*, New Series, Vol. XX, No. 78, May, 1953, p. 109. [2] *Op. cit.* [3] *Op. cit.*, p. 41.
[4] *Principles of Economics*, p. 94. [5] *Ibid.*, p. 95. [6] *Ibid.*, p. 96.

12. We reach the situation in which progressive taxation is thought to be justified on the grounds that 'we should tax what can be spared'.[1] But the argument does not end there, for Pigou, as it seems to me, explicitly worked his way into the field of redistribution theory. He said, 'it is evident that any transference of income from a relatively rich man to a relatively poor man of similar temperament, since it enables more intense wants to be satisfied at the expense of less intense wants, must increase the aggregate sum of satisfaction. The old 'law of diminishing utility' thus leads securely to the proposition: Any cause which increases the absolute share of real income in the hands of the poor, provided that it does not lead to a contraction in the size of the national dividend from any point of view, will, in general, increase economic welfare.'[2] Again, and with rather more force, 'We must not hesitate, therefore, to conclude that, so long as the dividend as a whole is not diminished, any increase, within wide limits, in the real income enjoyed by the poorer classes, at the expense of an equal decrease in that enjoyed by the richer classes, is practically certain to involve an addition to economic welfare.'[3] And, if we should want any more convincing, there is this final pronouncement. 'Among other measures of inequality the most familiar is the mean square deviation from the mean. With that criterion it can be proved that, assuming similarity of temperament among the members of the community, a diminution in the inequality of distribution *probably*, though not necessarily, increases the aggregate sum of satisfaction.'[4]

13. In this context perhaps we should remember that Marshall wanted the State 'to use its powers for promoting such economic and social adjustments as will make for the well-being of the people at large'.[5] At any rate, here we have most of the story to show us the influence of economic ideas on the progressive principle and we cannot fail to see that with the development of social aims, income redistribution has become a secondary but important feature of direct taxation. Nevertheless, I doubt whether either

[1] Paley in 1830. Cf. Stamp's *Principles of Taxation*, p. 41.

[2] *The Economics of Welfare*, p. 89.

[3] *Ibid.*, p. 96.

[4] *Ibid.*, p. 97.

[5] *After-War Problems*, p. 317.

Marshall or Pigou looked much beyond transfers at the margins of incomes and I think we should especially notice Pigou's proviso concerning the diminution of the national income as a whole. Surely this is a point at which such taxation becomes inimical to the economic progress of the society, and in any case there is much to be said for the contention that the process of taking away should not proceed beyond the *legitimate* needs of the state, although to define legitimate in this connection would want some doing. However, I think we can concede that some limits should be placed on very high incomes, and plainly very low incomes are undesirable.

14. I think we must all concede that any direct tax upon incomes is only possible in a mature society with some stability of government. It must be fair and equitable, and reach over the whole body politic. In general, it is desirable that a direct tax should be paid as near to the receipt of the income, on which it is assessed, as can be conveniently contrived. The current year basis of assessment always has much to commend it, and in my judgement the present delay in the time of payment of surtax is a cause of aggravation.

15. In a talk of this kind, I think we should also just notice a few questions of principle which are very much the concern of the central government. Stamp, having had much experience, put them in the following form. He said that:

The State as a tax gatherer has to ask and answer the following questions:

1. Is the proposed tax economical, or will it cost an unwarrantable amount to get in?
2. Is it within the powers of the administration for assessment and collection, or is it too full of difficulties to be workable? Allied thereto is the question:
3. Will it be specially open to evasion and provoke dishonesty?
4. Will the imposition of the tax tend to dry up the source of the tax, and so prove abortive for the Revenue?
5. Does it raise political difficulties at home and provoke unrest?
6. Does it raise international difficulties or provoke conflict with other taxing jurisdictions?[1]

[1] *Principles of Taxation*, pp. 103–4.

Most of these are obvious, but they bear re-statement. In particular, I direct your attention to number 3. If a tax is open to evasion then it is my view it is badly conceived. Legal evasion is not the same thing as dishonesty; it simply means that the implications of the tax were not properly thought out.

16. And now for a few general topics, and perhaps a few ideas, relevant to the whole discussion. I cannot help feeling that the present level of direct taxation on enterprise profits is so limiting enterprise savings that there is less inclination to embark upon new ventures. The development of new lines is always marked by some uncertainty, and surely there is less propensity to be venturesome or progressive, and so to face uncertainty, when enterprise savings are restricted. Thus, I hazard the view that in circumstances of high direct taxation a fore-known existence of profits is rather more likely to bring about increased operating costs than resourceful asset formation, and as I think we all sense, resourceful asset or capital formation is essential if we are to hold our own in world markets. Moreover, enterprise always has regard for revenue earning assets whereas collective asset formation is so often too devoted to considerations of security and long-run welfare.

17. A high direct taxation of enterprise profits which disregards the accounting implications of changing money values not only damps down progress, but can encroach upon business stability at existing levels of productivity. Shipping companies, in particular, are most sensitive to these effects. I quote from a speech of the chairman of the Union-Castle Mail Steamship Company to illustrate the point.

Our Wear and Tear relief from taxation is based upon the actual first cost of the ships. . . . There has not been much imagination in the mental processes of those who have governed us in regard to the conundrum as to how industry is going to find the money for the necessary replacing of old plant, seeing they have prevented us from making anything like adequate provision to meet that requirement by refusing to relieve us of the penalizing effect of taxation on moneys set aside for that purpose . . . It surely cannot be over-simplification to suggest that sums definitely earmarked—frozen if need be—for rehabilitation of shipping fleets should be free from all taxation, on the clear understanding that the moment they are used for any other purpose they become subject to the full measure of taxation at the rates then currently ruling.[1]

I know that by now this argument has become all too familiar. What is not so familiar is that normal quantities of stocks essential to the operating activity of a continuing enterprise involve fixed commitments of capital just as much as items of plant, and should be so treated when it comes to the assessment of enterprise profits. Surely, whatever the revenue requirements of the State, and the levels of rates necessary to meet them, it is time that the principles of direct taxation encompassed some economic principles of income measurement. I *do* feel that there is something serious in the statement of Sir George Christopher, 'that sums required to meet any enhancement in the costs of rejuvenating the Fleet . . . have to be found out of taxed profits or by borrowing or by both'.

18. Direct taxation is an inevitable concomitant of life in civilized society, but it can be pressed too far. Sir Henry Clay has recently reminded us that prices *secured* and profits *realized* are not the same things as prices *expected* and profits *planned*.[2] We know that modern enterprise is repeatedly engaged in the attempt to forecast outputs and prices, costs and profits, and, most importantly, the balance of profits over which management has the outlay decision, i.e. profits after taxation, and dividend distributions. Accordingly, entrepreneurs think of income tax as a material factor affecting prices. In the precise language of Sir Henry:

The industrialist thinks of income-tax as affecting prices, because it influences his decisions and therefore the volume of business and the terms on which it is undertaken. On a single deal the risk involved is balanced against the net gain to be expected, and, if the latter is reduced too far by tax, the deal will not be undertaken. On a project for increasing output, the cost of additional material and processing, adaptation and extension of plant, and other expenses, are all calculated; if the return to be expected *after tax* is not sufficient to cover these expenses,

[1] Speech by Sir George P. Christopher at the annual general meeting on May 28, 1953.

[2] 'A Note on Taxation and Prices', *Progress*, Spring, 1953 (Unilever Limited).

the project will not be worth undertaking. A tax on profits thus operates as a *tax on enterprise*, and tends to raise *the cost of enterprise.*

One other point. Our President is never done with his criticism of the present range and amount of government expenditure. He rightly regards such expenditure as an inflationary influence. The emphasis, he argues, is always on the amount to be raised by taxation rather than on the curtailment of expenditure. I do not think it is difficult to see that a too ready dependence on the revenue from taxation can very easily veil the presence of ineffective and excessive expenditure.

19. In our day we have seen the instrument of taxation used as one of the means of fostering a stable economy by way of the budget. You will remember the argument. It was the duty of the government to counteract economic forces making for instability, and to this end budget deficits were respectable, provided they promoted a full employment of resources and were kept down to an effective minimum. Keynes made it clear that consumption and capital (i.e. asset) formation, whether on government or private account, had to be kept in line with such real resources as were available. Thus, it came about that taxation fell into position as one of the policy expedients of a planned economy.[1] If the private sector failed to satisfy the real identity between savings and asset formation, then the public sector, with the aid of taxation, must redress the balance on whichever side it occurred. No doubt

[1] It is interesting to observe that in addition to intentional counter-cyclical changes brought about by government action, progressive taxation produces certain automatic effects. Thus, Mr. Lawrence H. Setzer dealing with the individual income tax in the United States remarks that: 'An increase in personal income before taxes tends to bring about a greater than proportional increase in income tax by subjecting the addition to the higher graduated rates and by adding to the number of persons on the tax rolls. The rise in the disposable, after-tax incomes of households is thereby moderated. Conversely, a decline in personal incomes brings about a greater than proportional reduction in income taxes and, therefore, a less than proportional decline in the disposable incomes of households. Beyond these automatic effects are the very substantial counter-cyclical changes in disposable personal incomes that Congress may now achieve by seemingly modest alterations in the level of personal exemptions and credits and in the tax rates applicable to the first bracket of taxable incomes.' (Thirty-third Annual Report, National Bureau of Economic Research, Inc., New York, May, 1953.)

all would have been well if public outlay had not proved so intractable, and international equilibrium so insecure.

20. I think we do well to remind ourselves that government outlay depends upon the real income of the nation, especially that part of it which comes through enterprise, and that, however we look at it, such outlay can only be met out of that which remains after the living necessities of the community have been satisfied.[1] This is but the bare bones of the problem. Private savings are vital, whether transferred to the central government or retained in private ownership, and, at bottom, it is for this reason that some have favoured an expenditure rather than an income tax. By far the greater part of private savings comes from corporate enterprises, but, as we have seen it is unlikely that such enterprises will be progressive if the greater part of their savings is delivered out of their jurisdiction. Moreover, a policy which sets the sights of individuals in terms of living necessities, and the provision of a minimum security, will end up by damping effort and restricting incomes. Defence expenditure in an unsettled world is inevitable, but the costs of a collective provider, and the costs of a central administration must never be allowed to endanger the free generation of incomes or the spirit of bold undertakings.

21. Fiscal policies then must have regard to the means available, and the effect on national product. It should never be forgotten that effort, savings, and the free acceptance of risks, are vital to our future welfare. Again, it should not be assumed that the State *always* has the best qualifications for spending. Nevertheless, methods of taxation have to be tested by trials and errors. If they sometimes go too far, at least thereby they mark some points of strain; points which may serve to aid the course of future generations.

[1] Much the same comment has been made by Professor R. C. Tress in his article 'Trends in Public Finance' (*Lloyds Bank Review*, July, 1953).

10

AUDITING THEORY

The substance of a paper given on 22nd October, 1954 to the Chartered Accountant Students' Society of Edinburgh

1. Auditing is an ancient practice bearing its own particular witness to the theological doctrine of original sin. It has always been directly concerned with matters of stewardship and accountability. The dishonest or careless steward was brought to a halt at the audit of his accounts. Away back in the past an auditor was a hearer; entries in accounts were read to him, and as an independent arbiter he approved or disapproved as he heard them. Thus, those who had the charge of other people's resources were required to give voice to their stewardship.

2. In principle, an audit is, and always has been, an independent third party examination of monetary and other records concerned with income and wealth. At first, and by the nature of things, this independent examination was a highly detailed affair very much preoccupied with the *bona fides* of incomings and outgoings. It persisted right up to my own time as an articled clerk, but with the development of accounting theory and practice, especially in the last thirty years, auditing ideas and methods have tended in part to move away from this meticulous inspection of an entity's recorded incomings and outgoings. Larger enterprises now have better control over the multitudinous transactions passing through their books of account. Almost imperceptibly, auditing theory has been brought to recognize the regularity and system which exists in economic life, and when it is not so much concerned with deliberate fraud it takes its cue from accounting theory and looks to the evidence supporting the presentation of a fair view of the epitomized transactions of an accounting entity both over time and at a defined point in time. The structure and form of accounts allied to significant disclosure, the existence of assets and liabilities, and the measurement of classified aggregates, have become as important, if not more important, than mere accountability for a

complete series of individual items of incoming and outgoing in succession.

3. Lord Justice Morris lecturing on *The Spirit of Justice* said recently that: 'The lawyer must seek to distinguish between the particular and the general. He has learned that the rules of a code of laws or of a legal system must as far as possible be uniform, certain and of general application.'[1] Equally the auditor must distinguish between the particular and the general. When auditing was absolutely concerned with the detailed examination of records then the particular was predominant. Nowadays, it is falling into place behind the general. And what are we to understand by the general in auditing? I suggest that the general theory of auditing must follow those general rules of an accounting system which as far as possible are uniform, certain and of general application.

4. In *Four Essays* I set out what I considered to be some of the general principles of a formal accounting system. I will touch on them here and comment as I go on their special relevance to auditing theory. There are two general economic concepts fundamental to the practice of accounting; they are *periodic income* and *wealth*. This involves a fundamental sifting of transactions into the categories of current and capital, or, if you prefer, those which end up in the profit and loss account and those which end up in the balance sheet. A modern auditor must take steps to see that this differentiation has been properly thought out, and carried out. Ofttimes this is a bothersome problem when we are dealing with expenditure. I give an example. It is not always easy to determine what borderline expenditure connected with fixed assets should be capitalized. Quite apart from verifying the mere *bona fides* of the outgoing, the auditor must consider whether such expenditure has added to the value of the asset, and whether it results in benefits which are deferable over time. He should inquire if such a particular outgoing has done anything to *increase the life* of the asset to which it is related, or to promote an increase in its *efficiency*, as measured either by output capacity and/or improved

[1] *The Spirit of Justice*, by the Rt. Honourable Lord Justice Morris. Haldane Memorial Lecture delivered at Birkbeck College, 1954.

product quality. If the expenditure has merely kept the asset in *working* order then it is a current cost.

5. Apart from the distinction between current and capital, transactions in accounts may be classified as real, financial, imputed and non-monetary. Without going into much detail, real transactions mainly refer to purchases and sales of goods and services, recorded at the times of transfers of title, at the prices then obtaining. Financial relates to transactions in debts and claims. Imputation refers to those transactions which do not arise from exchanges between entities, e.g. depreciation, and rent charges for owner-occupied buildings. Non-monetary means transactions in kind, e.g. directors' benefits received otherwise than in cash. As a matter of detail you should all be familiar with the auditing of real and financial transactions. You should know the kind of documents which are required to evidence real transactions, but you must always remember to investigate records of the physical movement of the goods which pass against the entries in the accounts. Financial transactions should give little cause for difficulty providing you remember that some transactions in debts and claims are limited by constitutional considerations. The auditing techniques relevant to both real and financial transactions are commonplace, and are to be found in any generally accepted text-book.

6. Imputed transactions call for the exercise of judgement and belong to another category, although I am afraid that for your present purposes I cannot guide you much beyond the accepted conventions. Thus, a modern auditor will need to be convinced that a proper method of depreciating fixed assets has been consistently followed from one period to another. He should satisfy himself that it conforms to a reasonable pattern of experienced technical factors, and if price factors have been taken account of he should judge their propriety and view the matter from the standpoint of an adequate disclosure in the final accounts. Rent charges for owner-occupied buildings can be tested by reference to net annual values. Non-monetary transactions are not so easily verified. For one thing, the physical records are apt to be imperfectly kept and therefore are not usually acceptable without the

support of substantiating answers to careful inquiries. Then again, there is a pricing problem which can only be dealt with if the auditor has some knowledge of, or calls for information on, the prices of similar goods which have been the subject of actual *exchange* transactions on a market around the same time.

7. I return to the bearing of accounting theory on auditing theory, and I want to bring to your notice two very simple propositions which are at the bottom of all final accounts required to be audited. The first says that in a given time period income is devoted to consumption expenditure and saving. The second says that saving is resolved in capital formation. We rarely find that companies and suchlike enterprises constituted for profit come within the ranks of final consumers, although occasionally professional auditors are concerned with the spending accounts of persons and estates. If we rule out consumption expenditure from the general run of commercial auditing, we are left with concepts of income, saving and capital. A proper accounting structure for a commercial enterprise will be generally expressed in a set of formally related accounts: a profit and loss account to measure period income, an appropriation account to show transfers of income and the measurement of saving, sometimes a 'sources and utilization of funds' statement primarily to show the application of saving, and a balance sheet to measure capital as a stock. I do not need to remind you of the importance of income measurement to an auditor who is concerned to see that the legal and financial constraints on income distribution have been properly observed. Quite apart from the intrinsic auditing principles of justification and verification, the modern auditor is getting in the situation where he is expected to take some responsibility for the structure and form of final accounts, and the conceptual measurements which such accounts are meant to give, although as things stand at present such things are very largely matters of convention and statute. It is usually said that accounts are matters of stewardship prepared for shareholders and proprietors, and as a consequence an auditor's responsibility to third parties who have incidentally relied upon those accounts lies in the grey land of legal obligation. I can

see the day coming, however, when accounts based on the kind of theory I have been putting to you will put the practice of auditing on a much more objective basis, such that an auditor will be expected to attest the objective reliability of the accounts and their conceptual measurements, but this is still some way off.

8. As we all know, companies are the most important entities with which the modern auditor has to do, and the Companies Act, 1948, has some rather vital regulations on the subject. The auditors' report must be attached to any circulated or published copies of the accounts. This report is addressed to members on the accounts examined and on all balance sheets, profit and loss accounts and group accounts, laid before the company. In general it states whether the auditors have obtained all necessary information, whether proper books have been kept, whether the balance sheet and profit and loss accounts are in agreement with the books, whether they present a true and fair view of the company's affairs, and whether they give the information required by the Act. As Professor Gower has recently pointed out, the disclosure philosophy regarded as the fundamental principle of investor protection, only works if the information disclosed can be safely taken as accurate. 'Unless checked by some independent authority this cannot be relied on; so far as the accounts are concerned the auditors are this independent authority.'[1]

9. Although the Companies Act is clear on the nature of auditors' duties we are still confronted with a measure of uncertainty in regard to the care and skill which they are to exercise in carrying out their duties. We all remember the famous judgement of Lopes, L. J., in the *Kingston Cotton Mill* case, but the reported cases referred to in our text-books are for the most part old and it is doubtful if they can be wholly relied upon for guidance in the future. The general principle is plain. An auditor must act with that skill, care and caution which a reasonably competent, careful and cautious auditor would use. Professional standards are rising, and notwithstanding the dictum in the *Kingston Cotton Mill* case Professor Gower suggests that 'it is coming to be accepted that an

[1] *The Principles of Modern Company Law*, by L. C. B. Gower (London: Stevens & Sons Ltd., 1954), p. 450.

auditor should not rely wholly on the honesty and accuracy of others even as regards taking stock, and that he should at least satisfy himself that it has been taken on sound principles and, probably, that he should carry out a spot check of at least one sample item'.[1] It is not difficult to see the anomaly in a meticulous vouching of petty cash expenditure when stock valuations have been cursorily regarded.

10. I spoke earlier about regularity and system in economic life, a regularity and system which is well marked in a firm's accounting methods. This leads me to the related subjects of internal control and sampling tests. We know that the end of an audit is only achieved by a responsible and orderly examination of records, but if a modern auditor of a reasonably large-scale undertaking is to exhaust the possibilities of bringing to light *all* cases of dishonesty and fraud then he must attempt a thoroughly detailed examination, not missing out anything. For the great majority of such concerns this would involve a prohibitive cost, a cost which would be out of proportion to the benefits achieved. It has therefore come about that the modern auditor of sizeable enterprises has first to proceed by acquiring a personal familiarity with the procedures and methods of the accounting system; he must know their functions and their limitations, he must assure himself that they are so designed as to control errors and irregularities and he must know that they are working as they were planned.[2] If he is thoroughly satisfied on the adequacy and effectiveness of the system he can then resort to sampling tests, but he should never forget that the implications of such entries as he does meticulously examine must be carefully thought about before they are passed. He must especially see to it that the control elements of the system of accounting are such that undisclosed transactions are well-nigh impossible, and while we are on this question of undisclosed transactions we all know how necessary it is to consult the minute-books of companies. In recent years there have been a

[1] *Ibid.*, p. 452.

[2] Cf. the references to 'Proper Evaluation of the Examinee's Existing Internal Control for Reliance Thereon by the Auditor' in *Generally Accepted Auditing Standards*, Special Report by the Committee on Auditing Procedure of the American Institute of Accountants (1954).

number of statistical suggestions involving sampling methods as applied to auditing test checks. It seems to me that these methods very largely relate to the discovery of errors and irregularities in recording, and therefore I regard them as more peculiar to internal control or internal auditing than to the independent audit. I quote from some remarks which I made about this to a conference of statisticians at Oxford in 1952:

A certain amount has been written about sampling methods as applied to auditing test checks. In this context I must record my view that fraudulent entries, or a lack of entries presupposing fraud, in books of account, usually turn up when and where they are unsuspected, with all the characteristics of the unexpected. I am, therefore, sufficiently old-fashioned to prefer the examination of a selected series of entries which is both complete and continuous in itself, in order to secure that nothing at random has matured within that range. I am inclined to think that the selection of the period is more a matter of auditing experience than of technical analysis, though I do see that a sequential sampling plan used systematically has advantages where the records of large industrial entities are made the subjects of continuous audits. The trouble is that apart from mere mechanist slips, slips which should be virtually non-existent in these days of highly developed recording, no error is really acceptable to an auditor as an *error* until its motive has been thoroughly probed.

11. In a recent publication of the American Institute on *Generally Accepted Auditing Standards*, it is said that an extensive insight into a system of control can be obtained by investigating a series of related transactions:

For example, review of the data supporting the various steps arising from a certain requisition for materials, including the preparation of the purchase order, the record of the receipt of the material, the approval of the voucher for payment, payment therefor, and tracing the transactions to the particular accounts, is often more revealing than the examination of vouchers or checks for a specified period of time.[1]

12. A great deal of judgement is required of the independent auditor in selecting adequate samples of entries for testing the

[1] p. 33.

validity of a firm's accounts. For example, the modern auditor should pay attention to the system in force for plant construction authorization and the system for operating budgets; and I should not regard it as outside his province to call for the budgets relevant to the period of his audit. In most cases inventories present problems, and whilst it may be very necessary to restrict oneself to sampling procedures in this context, it is plainly quite inadequate to apply such techniques to the verification of investments.[1] Where verification and checking is a difficult matter because of the complexities of recording, then it is essential that the independent auditor should concentrate his attention at this point.

13. Internal check and control are especially related to the subject of mechanized accounting. You may remember that the Report of the Mechanized Accounting Sub-Committee of the Taxation and Financial Relations Committee of The Institute of Chartered Accountants in England and Wales made the point that:

> Audit checks should, more than ever, be directed to testing the principles of the accounting system (including the internal check) and its practical operation. If the principles are sound and applied effectively, the auditor will be able to dispense with a considerable amount of detailed routine checking. The soundness and efficiency of the control system are of much greater importance than the mechanical operation of the machine or the hole in a card. If it is established by means of test-checks that the control records do prove the arithmetical accuracy of the ledgers, then it becomes possible for the auditor to vouch, by means of code references, direct from prime documents to the ledgers instead of through the intermediary of a day-book. Direct vouching in this way has distinct auditing advantages, particularly in vouching the private and nominal ledgers.[2]

14. It should be especially remembered that transactions which do not lend themselves to the normal routine of the accounting system should receive special attention from the independent auditor. While we are on the subject of mechanized systems I think we should notice one of its most serious dangers. Again

[1] p. 35.
[2] *Mechanised Accounting and the Auditor*, March 1949, p. 16.

I quote from the Report of the Mechanized Accounting Sub-Committee:

There is also a danger—one of the most serious dangers in any mechanized system—of prime documents or punched cards being miscoded and resulting in the transaction being guided from the start through the wrong channel, a type of error which may be difficult to locate. In general, it will be found that an internal check must be imposed in some form on all or most of the postings, particularly in regard to allocation, but to a large extent this can be achieved by breaking down the controls into suitable subsections, thus narrowing the risk of errors remaining undetected.[1]

15. It has been said in some quarters that modern auditing is almost wholly devoted to questions of stewardship, that this in itself is a negative affair and that the modern auditor should develop positive techniques which will enable him to give an opinion on the efficiency with which the accounting entity has been conducted. Efficiency audits may or may not prove a desirable development, but I should like to say that in my judgement there is nothing very unusual about them, only their name. Investigations have always been a common feature of professional work, but I suggest they are different in category from the kind of audit which is required by the Companies Act, 1948, and they should not be thought of in the same context. In the normal stewardship audit, 'scrutiny of vouchers and records and the follow-up and explanations of abnormal items remain the foundation of the audit procedure'.[2] Verification and a careful regard for methods of valuation, within the limits of accepted principles and conventions, are still the keynotes of modern auditing standards.

[1] p. 18. [2] p. 19.

II

A FORMAL REVIEW OF SOCIAL ACCOUNTING

The substance of a paper given on 28th January, 1955 to the Liverpool Economic and Statistical Society

1. I approach the subject of social accounting from the standpoint of an accountant. If it should seem strange that such a statement is necessary on a subject which includes accounting as one of its terms, then I must reply that, in fact, the modern idea of accounting for society began in the field of applied economics. This, of itself, should serve to show us that the basic concepts of economics and accounting are not so different. Indeed, when I come to read Schumpeter's *History of Economic Analysis*,[1] I cannot avoid the suspicion that had there been an accountant familiar with the moral thinking of the medieval schoolmen on income and wealth, who chanced to live at or before the same time as Adam Smith, and possessed his stature; then by now we might have established accounting within the social sciences. But we know this was not the case.

2. Gilbert and Stone have said that:

> Social accounting, in the sense of the quantitative description of an economic system in terms of its constituent transactions suitably classified and aggregated, is in practical terms a development of the Second World War and the post-war period. A technique of this kind, with its emphasis on consistency, was needed as soon as estimates of income, expenditure and other aggregates of transactions came to be made and compared, for without a clear understanding of the relationships between these magnitudes, all sorts of misconceptions were apt to arise from the statistical discrepancies that appeared in the estimates.[2]

Quite so; but as it seems to me, the whole pattern of social accounting has been based on its convenience for statistical

[1] New York, Oxford University Press, 1954; London, George Allen & Unwin Ltd.

[2] 'Recent developments in national income and social accounting', by Milton Gilbert and Richard Stone, *Accounting Research*, January 1954, p. 1.

description, and for this reason I think there are some recent presentations which are too complex. A variety of detail finds its way into the accounts, and sometimes the structure of the accounts is unstable. When these presentations fall into the hands of those who are inexpert in the vagaries of the technique it is always possible that the significance of fundamental estimates will be missed. As we know, in the present way of doing things, statistically derived estimates of aggregate transactions are put into accounting form because of the convenience of the double-entry constraint. In this paper we shall try to review the subject another way round, and for this purpose we shall start with a ground plan of *accounting* theory.

3. Accounting is so much a part of the business of everyday life that some acquaintance with its concepts and forms, as well as its uses, is very nearly an essential part of the equipment of most people who are engaged in earning a living from industry and commerce. It is, therefore, appropriate to suggest that if social accounting is to be commonly understood it should conform to the accepted patterns of private accounting. In one way or another, most definitions of private accounting begin by treating it as an orderly way of collecting, classifying and aggregating money facts about exchanges of goods and services and transfers of *value*.

4. The primary functions of accounts, social no less than private, can be listed in the following way:

i. To give a clear record of and to measure periodic *income* from economic activity.
ii. To measure changes in the make-up of periodic incomes.
iii. To show how far economic activity has been effectively carried out.
iv. To reveal the effect and measurement of income transfers.
v. To control outlay over time by measurements of spending and saving.
vi. To show the uses to which saving has been put and to measure capital changes over time.
vii. To give an inventory of assets and liabilities and to measure the wealth and credit standing of an entity of account.

5. These functions are based upon the fundamental economic conceptions of production, consumption, wealth and adding to wealth, which are the genuine sources for accounting notions of income, spending, capital and saving. Thus, it has been said that:

> An economic system embraces three basic forms of activity which we may term production, consumption and adding to wealth. Production may be defined as bringing into being goods and services on which members of the community or the community as a whole, through its elected representatives, set a valuation. Consumption may be defined as the using up and wearing out of the fruits of production and adding to wealth may be defined as the preservation of the fruits of production for consumption or for contributing to consumption later on.[1]

The point which has to be made, however, is that economic activity always requires the preparation of accounts, for as long as men exchange goods and services they will want accounts to give them views of their transactions. Accounting, then, is a means of systematizing economic transactions to help us to understand the workings of those agents in society which create incomes, spend incomes, and add to or subtract from wealth. By planned arrangements of aggregates it *unifies* a great number of diverse transactions, and thereby succinctly explains both the utilization of, and state of, resources, which assists those who have to make decisions about economic activities and their financial implications.

6. Accounting is essential to all economic thinking conducted from a factual basis, because it gives a factual record in an orderly manner. In the world of practical affairs we can only interpret what is happening when we know something about the facts. As we have suggested, the ordering of those facts depends upon our conception of a few significant economic variables. Schumpeter has made the point that

> we have a strong scientific interest in reducing the number of the economic variables with which we have to deal.

[1] *Functions and Criteria of a System of Social Accounting*, by Richard Stone. Income and Wealth Series I (1951). Bowes & Bowes Ltd., Cambridge.

He goes on to say that

> if we tried to write down the equations that determine the static equilibrium of millions of firms and households, we should never accomplish the task. In particular, we could never marshal the statistics that would be the necessary complement of such a system. This suggests the idea of reducing the number of variables to a few great social aggregates. This idea is very old. From the first, economists have tried to reason on national income, national sum total of wages and the like. But it was only during the last quarter of a century that this idea has been systematically followed up. It is clear that we should be in a much better position to apply theory to statistics and statistics to theory if we could, for some purposes or for all, confine ourselves to such variables as National Income, National Consumption and Investment, Quantity of Money, Employment, and Interest Rates. Analysis which attempts to do so is called *Macroanalysis* (R. Frisch). Because the National Income is the central variable in which we are particularly interested, it is also called *Income Analysis*.[1]

To this statement I add another, taken from Irving Fisher's book on *The Nature of Capital and Income*:

> Careful examination shows that accounting is, at bottom, not a mere makeshift but a complete, consistent and logical system. When thus conceived and understood, it will be seen to be of importance, not alone to the accountant but also to the economist.[2]

7. In social, as in private accounting, we are primarily interested in income formation, spending, saving and capital formation. The functions of accounting and our general understanding of economic events suggests that what is always wanted is a simple set of related accounts, one to measure periodic income and its changes, two to show its transfer and disposition, three to record outlay, four to explain the application of retained income or saving, its effect upon wealth and capital changes, and five to measure and portray in balance sheet form those real and financial resources which together make up the wealth of an entity. It is one of my

[1] *History of Economic Analysis*, by Joseph A. Schumpeter (New York, Oxford University Press, 1954; London: George Allen & Unwin Ltd.), p. 1143.

[2] *The Nature of Capital and Income*, by Irving Fisher (New York: The Macmillan Co., 1919), p. 140.

complaints about existing social accounting presentations that this simplicity is not always readily discernible.

8. Those of you who are familiar with my booklet on *Accounting Developments*[1] will know that I had something to say about this when reviewing the simplified system of national accounts which was designed to assist in comparing the structure of transactions in countries which were members of the Organization for European Economic Co-operation. You may remember that I did not like the national revenue and expenditure account because it was both a consolidated current account and a consolidated resting or capital change account; a double piece of compression which seemed to be engaged in to get at total figures for gross national revenue and gross national expenditure. I have never had much inclination for this gross terminology, but the real point about the criticism was the fact that the accounts themselves did not keep to the measurement of those few linking variables which we have regarded as significant. I also commented on the absence of a balance sheet, but qualified this comment by recognizing the formidable nature of the task especially in regard to the classification and valuation of real assets.

9. Once you accept the idea of a few significant variables, the accounting statement of them is logical and consistent when they emerge within a double-entry framework. We know that double-entry recording is fundamental to accounting theory, for if there is a receiver of money or its equivalent, then there is also a payer. This explains why it always shows itself in those planned arrangements, either of transactions or aggregates, called accounts, and thereby imparts to them a measure of coherence. Accounts must balance, and it is the great merit of the double-entry principle that it so provides a check on the disposition of recorded transactions. Once a transaction has been noted in a double-entry system, formally maintained, it cannot be lost sight of. Fundamentally, then, we should think of double-entry as a logical means of dealing with transactions in the order in which they have occurred, a mechanism for handling continuous and verifiable

[1] Reprint Series No. 4. Incorporated Accounts' Research Committee for the Stamp-Martin Professor.

data. In fact, the double-entry procedure is an expression of exchange. Exchange is at the centre of economic life and involves a receiver and a giver, and an incoming and outgoing, both real and financial, at the same time. Thus, economic processes, whatever their magnitudes, have balancing properties, and such processes are not properly portrayed quantitatively unless these are revealed. Nevertheless it is important to remember that accounting presentations are partly descriptive and may not necessarily express causal relationships, although I do tend to regard output estimates as partly generating causative relationships.

10. A second basic principle of accounting which should be mentioned here, relates exchange and other transactions to an entity, or, as some prefer to think, a transactor. I do not altogether favour the term 'transactor' in this context, because it suggests the economic dealings of a real or legal person, and that would limit the scope of accounts. The word 'entity' has a wider meaning which is more significant for accounting theory. Although both terms are used in the following statement, the distinction between them is clear. Thus, we cannot begin to shape accounts until we have conceived either the units of organized activity or the transactor whose history and condition we wish to measure and portray in financial terms. Plainly we must look at the transactions which take place under one roof, whatever that roof may be. I therefore regard the entity notion of accounting theory as primary. If you keep to the provisos I am about to mention you can make the entity what you will. It may be a firm, a person, or a company; it may be legal or domestic, a group or an individiual; it may ascend or descend the hierarchy of economies to be limited at will by political, industrial or natural boundaries; but whatever province we do choose to account for we know that it must have a real existence, and it must be significant for the purposes which finally resolve the structure of all accounts: namely the measurement of periodic income and the measurement of wealth.

In social accounting the lesser sector entities, as a minimum, are usually functionally classified as producers, governments, households and sometimes regions; the greater entity is, of course, the nation.

11. Sector accounting as now conceived within social accounting is not quite so new as some would have us believe. For example, I have seen recently a reproduction of *The General Ledger of the Kingdom of Sweden*, dated 1623. I understand that this general ledger of 1623

> marks a revolutionary change in the financial administration of Sweden —the application of the double-entry book-keeping system to government accounts. It is the oldest double-entry account book of any kind known to exist in that country.

Moreover, it appears that

> this reform was one of the products of the reorganization program carried out in the reign of King Gustav Adolf (1611–1632). The instrument for financial control

—and this is the interesting point in the context of our present discussion—

> had already been created by Gustav Vasa in 1539 in the form of a permanent Chamber for the central financial administration. Under Gustav Adolf, this Chamber (Kammaren) had two departments, one for the Treasury and one for accounts. The latter, at first concerned mainly with the audit of local agents of the Crown, was soon delegated new tasks. The first was to prepare annual government budgets of revenue and expenditure, beginning in 1619. The second was to set up a new system of central account books, *primarily intended to give a comprehensive view of the revenue and expenditure of the entire Kingdom.*[1] This idea had already been used in a very simple form on at least two earlier occasions during the sixteenth century. The epoch-making character of the seventeenth-century application of the concept lay in the decision to adopt the double-entry system for this and other accounts.

It is clear from this that social accounting concepts and ideas have an early origin, and even more remarkable, as I think, is the fact that the accounts of the central government sector were to be based on actual double-entry records and not statistically derived.

Another point of interest which I think should be specially

[1] Italics mine.

marked having regard to the impetus given to modern social accounting development in the Netherlands, is the fact that as

the intended system was very little known or practised in Sweden at that time, the government in 1623 called in a prominent Dutch merchant, Abraham Cabiljan, to carry out the reorganization.

It seems that

Cabiljan was born in Leyden in 1571 and had formerly been a merchant in Amsterdam. He lived in Sweden from 1607 to 1617 and from 1621 to his death in 1645. In Sweden he held several prominent positions in the service of the government. He apparently had had no previous experience in the field of government accounting, but he was known to be an outstanding administrator and an expert in double-entry book-keeping. He may have been familiar with the ideas of the Dutch mathematician, Simon Stevin, who, in books published in 1608, suggested the use of double-entry book-keeping for government accounts. This cannot be proved, however, since there are many differences in technique between Stevin's proposals and the ledger of 1623.[1]

This piece of information is even more fascinating to someone, like myself, who recently attended the Accountants' Day of the Netherlands Institute, at which Professor Witteveen made considerable use of social accounting concepts in his deductions from the identity between national income and imports on the one hand and consumption, investment, government expenditure, and exports on the other hand. His general thesis had some bearing on the functions of accounting in their social context, especially the income and capital change accounts, for he argued that

the susceptibility of economic life to business cycles depends on the degree to which a primary change in the stream of incomes develops.

He said that the two chief factors determining the extent of this cumulative development were

the degree to which a change in incomes leads to a change in the demand for home-produced consumption goods (the marginal consumption

[1] These quotations have been taken from an English Summary relating to a recent treatise by Per V. A. Hanner, published by Förlagsaktiebolaget Affärsekonomi in recognition of Professor Oskar Sillén's service on the editorial board of the publishing company.

quota); and the degree to which a change in the production of consumption goods can lead to a change in investments.

He also made the point, familiar to most of us, that

the level of the national income is now determined to a far greater extent by government expenditure.[1]

12. I think that most economists who have seriously considered the development of social accounting would claim that consolidated national accounts do provide a certain factual background from which, as an example, it is possible to tell the extent to which a national economy is dependent upon foreign trade. With the further development of input-output analysis they would also see the probable matching of the supply of and demand for productive resources in the immediate future, and the financing of it in the form of a budget. Nevertheless, our understanding of the behaviour of national aggregates is usually clearer if the accounts which measure them are relatively simple, and this seems to me to fit in with the statement that

comprehensiveness of statistical data and the elaboration of relationships expressing economic behaviour assume a greater importance the smaller the number of variables that are determined in advance by acts of public policy.[2]

Social accounting simplicity is thus made partly dependent upon acts of public policy, but, equally public policy will not be reasonably understood without social accounting simplicity.

13. Another issue which needs to be made clear in all accounting, private no less than social, is the distinction between the real and the financial. The financial end of things can be thought of as an outer band protecting the real, and all ideas about working capital should be looked upon in this light. Fundamentally, it is real resources and their utilization which are important, but real

[1] *Stellingen van Prof. H. J. Witteveen insake het onderwerp: is de wereldeconomie minder conjunctuurgevoelig gewarden?* Nederlands Instituut van Accountants, Accountantsdag, 1954.

[2] Statistical Office of the United Nations, August 1952. *A System of National Accounts and Supporting Tables.* Report prepared by a Committee of National Income Experts appointed by the Secretary-General. New York. p. 8.

resources cannot be acquired, put into use, or kept in use without finance.

14. As we have seen, in considering a design for the accounts of society we are implicated in the nature and significance of the accounting exercise itself, including some of its principles, the concepts of structure and form, and the concepts of measurement and behaviour. We have first to deal with primary accounts and the relationships between the aggregate categories included in those accounts. Thereafter we have to look at difference accounts and the relationships between the aggregate categories included in those accounts. In setting up these accounts we should concentrate on clear and simple forms, so that categories for aggregates are few and essential. In this way their significance can be quickly taken in and understood.

15. I now turn to what might be called a generally accepted presentation of social accounts, but before looking at this in detail, I just want to mention that I shall not be specifically considering the social accounts of the United Kingdom as given in the Blue Book on *National Income and Expenditure, 1946–53.*[1] Nevertheless, let me say at once that I do regard this particular publication as a very well formulated piece of work, especially having regard to the source-material available.

Gilbert and Stone have told us that the *Standardized System of National Accounts* used by the Organization for European Economic Co-operation divides the transactions of an economy into those main groups which are important for analytical purposes:

> purchases and sales of goods and services, payments and receipts for factor services, payments and receipts of unilateral transfers and transactions involving financial claims. Appropriate classifications for each of these main categories are provided.[2]

The transactions are entered on six accounts,

> which provide the minimum division of the economy into sectors needed for analytical purposes and which also yield the main national income aggregates.

[1] *National Income and Expenditure, 1946–53.* H.M. Stationery Office, August 1954.

[2] 'Recent developments in national income and social accounting', by Milton Gilbert and Richard Stone. *Accounting Research*, January 1954, pp. 5 and 6.

I want to review these accounts and to offer some comments in the light of the kind of economic accounting theory which I think is worth following. You will remember that we have already emphasized conceptual measurements of income formation, spending, saving and capital formation, because these are traditional in the world of enterprise, both to the formulation and understanding of accounts. All accountants have been schooled in the significance of periodical measurements of profits and their make-up and the importance to be ascribed to undistributed income.

16. The first of the six accounts noted by Gilbert and Stone is called a National Product and Expenditure account. It is clearly designed to bring out the gross national product at market prices and the gross national expenditure at market prices. Although it is useful to have these gross figures of product and expenditure, I do not find it easy to regard them as of first importance. My order for accounting understanding would be Income, Appropriation, Outlay and Capital. The National Product and Expenditure account is virtually a consolidated Outlay account. On the left-hand side we have national income plus depreciation and other operating provisions plus indirect taxes less subsidies, to give gross national product at market prices. On the right-hand side we have consumers' expenditure on goods and services plus gross domestic asset formation plus [sales of goods and services to the rest of the world and factor income payments from the rest of the world less purchases of goods and services from the rest of the world and factor income payment to the rest of the world] to give gross national expenditure at market prices.

As is customary with economist-trained social accountants, the account seems to be organized on a receipts and payments basis, whereas an accountant would expect income to be credited and expenditure debited. I have been into this several times before, and there is little point in pursuing it here. Nevertheless, it does seem to me that the account would be plainer if the depreciation provision was shown as a disclosed inset deduction from gross domestic asset formation, and if the figures for indirect taxes and subsidies were shown as disclosed inset adjustments to consumers, expenditure on goods and services. I recognize that this would impair the gross total concepts at market prices, but there would be a distinct gain in understanding, as it seems to me, in setting forth a clear view of the outlay of income. Measurements of gross national product and gross national expenditure at market prices could be easily detailed by way of subsidiary information. The important relationships in outlay are those which relate income to consumption expenditure, and income to saving, especially if we are interested in periodic standard relationships. As a consequence, an outlay change account would be valuable so that we could see the changing nature of these relationships.

17. The second account which Gilbert and Stone give in their minimum division of the economy is the National Income account. I think it should have been the first account. It is meant to explain the make-up of national income in minimum terms, but in doing so it strays into appropriations of income in concertina fashion. Thus, the national income is given as compensation of employees plus income from property and entrepreneurship accruing to households, etc., plus saving of corporations plus direct taxes on corporations plus government income from property and entrepreneurship less interest on the public debt. Compensation of employees is clear enough, but as an accountant, I cannot feel happy with even a minimum presentation if it is without an operating account for enterprise or entrepreneurship. As things stand, enterprise income has to be deduced from four items: namely income from property and entrepreneurship accruing to households, etc., saving of corporations, direct taxes on corporations, and government income from property and entrepreneurship; to say the least of it a rather back-handed way of doing things. I recognize that paucity of statistical resources has something to do with this, but as a formal point I should have preferred enterprise income to be separately stated in the consolidated income account and saving to be regarded as a balance on consolidated outlay account, and direct taxes to be shown as a transfer payment in a consolidated appropriation account. The present compression does not make for accounting understanding because it is statistically conceived.

18. If sufficient statistical resources are available there is everything to be said for the production of sub-operating accounts designed to show the behaviour of different types of organization, but in any event it does seem to me that even a minimum presentation should include an aggregated operating account for enterprise or entrepreneurship prepared with the object of recording the value added by productive economic activity. I say, aggregated, despite the suggestion of double-counting, because I am concerned to emphasize the importance of standard relationships. A very simple form of this account, restricted to the barest minimum of 'make-up' information, could be given on the lines of the combined operating account for public corporations included in the Blue Book on *National Income and Expenditure, 1946–53*, as Table 25. I give an example of what I mean below:

Purchases of goods and services	x		Sales of goods and services ...	x
Changes in inventories... ...	x			
	—	x		
Net output or value added ...		x		
		—		—
		x		x
		=		=
Income from employment ...		x	Net output or value added ...	x
Rent		x	Subsidies*	x
Taxes on expenditure* (e.g. rates, motor vehicles and catering licences)		x		
Depreciation		x		
		—		
		x		
Operating income		x		
		—		—
		x		x
		=		=

* In strict theory we could regard these items as transfers into and out of operating income.

From this style of operating account we can devise over-all standard relationships between the consumption of purchased goods and services on the one hand and sold goods and services on the other hand, between income from employment and net output, and between rent and depreciation and net output. It is true that these are only financial relationships between aggregates which cover up a number of different conceptual categories on the expenditure side, nevertheless they do give us some ideas about production if they are supported by a difference account showing the changes from one accounting period to another.[1] A comparison of periodical standard relationships with change relationships of the same order would be especially interesting. Another interesting development of periodical standard relationships could come about by way of a comparison deduced from the aggregated operating accounts of private enterprise and government enterprise. In fact, when we are considering operating behaviour patterns of this order, standard relationships might be regarded as circumstantial sanctions to evidence the effective use of resources in income generation.

19. The third account given by Gilbert and Stone in their minimum presentation is called a Consolidated Appropriation account for General Government. There is little that need be said about this account except that outlay is included in the appropriation. Thus, on the left-hand side, government current expenditure on goods and services plus subsidies is included with items for interest on the public debt, current transfers to households, etc. (net), current transfers to the rest of the world, and saving of government to give one total for current expenditure and saving of general government. I cannot altogether see why *this total* is especially significant, except that it is the balancing counterpart to a right-hand side total for current revenue of general government, which, incidentally, includes an item for current transfers from the rest of the world. My real quibble with the showing of this account is that *all* transfers should be separately dealt with in a sectional part of the account before outlay is considered. A similar view might be taken in regard to the fourth account, described as a consolidated appropriation account for households and private non-profit institutions—and surely compensation of employees plus entrepreneurship income might be sub-totalled to give a figure of income from operating activity. I have always found a formal difficulty in accepting the compression

[1] See *Accounting Dynamics—II.*

of outlay and appropriation in one account, and I do not care for a heading which conjoins dissimilar groups like households and private non-profit institutions.

20. Accounts five and six are straightforward. Number five presents consolidated capital transactions. If I have a point about it at all, I should wish to see depreciation treated as an inset deduction from gross domestic asset formation. It always seems to me odd that depreciation and other operating provisions should be included with saving and other items to give a total for the gross addition to national wealth. In this context, I cannot but regard the use of the term 'gross' as somewhat misleading. Account number six in the Gilbert and Stone presentation is a Consolidated account for the Rest of the World which, because of its simplicity and clarity, does not call for comment. There is a great deal to be said on the score of understanding for a minimum system of accounts and entries, because, as Gilbert and Stone remark,

> it has the advantage of being capable of greater elaboration within its given framework by countries whose statistical resources make such elaboration feasible.

21. Standardization of social accounts is obviously a desirable ideal, more especially if we remember that, as in private accounting, the measurement of operating income, however derived, is a vital aggregate; in fact it is the whole issue in national income measurement. Gilbert and Stone foresee the development of standardization along three lines, with which it would be impossible to quarrel.

> The first is . . . elaboration . . . to embrace additional aspects of social accounting, such as input-output statistics, capital accounts by sectors, and balance sheets for sectors and for the whole economy. The second is to provide more satisfactory operational definitions of various components of the national accounts, especially those which present particular conceptual difficulties, such as gross capital formation and depreciation. The third is improvement in the statistical comparability of national accounts estimates.

22. Although I regard input-output analysis as an accounting development, I think that, to be of real use, it is best considered in

the field of both economic and accounting dynamics. In my view an important approach to this subject could come by way of deductions from periodical input-output change accounts, but I will not pursue this suggestion here. In private accounting, some importance is attached to the relationship between operating income and the value of operating assets employed, but if we gave any significance to this ratio in social accounting it would mean a much more decided development in balance sheet estimates than has so far proved possible. Gilbert and Stone on this question sum up thus:

In the rapid spread of social accounting over the past twelve years, attention has been concentrated almost exclusively on flows as opposed to stocks. The resulting accounting systems are incomplete, since they lack sector and national balance sheets. This common omission is not difficult to understand in practical terms. For, on the one hand, the construction of balance sheets involves a number of conceptual problems which do not have to be considered in constructing flow accounts and, on the other hand, balance sheets involve statistical data which, in most countries, are not at present available. Recent work on economectric models, however, serves to emphasize the importance of a knowledge of balance sheet items, both in the study of the relationship between product and capital formation and in a general formulation of the relationship between consumption and income. From the point of view of the utility of the social accounts, therefore, as from that of their formal completeness, the present position is unsatisfactory and constitutes a challenge to those engaged in social accounting.

Some attention has been given to this problem, and in that connection I should especially like to make mention of the work of Rijken van Olst, Korn and Oomens in the Netherlands and Goldsmith in the United States.

23. One is frequently asked about the *practical* uses of social accounts. Well, we surely need to know whether the signs are good or bad in the country's internal economy, and in its external position. Are we establishing our sources of external credit? What is happening to our external balance and our exports? Are personal and corporate savings increasing or decreasing? Is *real* national income increasing, and, if so, how is it being applied—in

increased consumption or increased saving? I quote from a recent speech of the Chancellor of the Exchequer.

I have always emphasized that the best way—and in the long run the only way—to ease the strains on the economy was to expand production. Between 1950 and 1953 the national product increased by about 7 per cent in real terms. It was this increase in our output which enabled us to carry out the very heavy increase in defence expenditure, which required about half of it. Much of the remainder went on housing, and very little to consumption.

If production goes on expanding (as it is still doing) and with the big rise in the defence programme behind us, we should be able to devote future increases in output to investment and to raising the standard of living. The rate at which we increase the scale and efficiency of our production year by year will decide our position in the world.'[1]

I close with only one proposition, which always seems to me relevant to the kind of aggregate measures we have been considering. Whatever values we may regard as determining the goal of mankind, it is always desirable to set our sights to an expanding economy, and to judge this in terms of an increasing *real* income, and an increasing *real* wealth accumulation. I know that this will appear to many as a trite and over-simplified abstraction which fails to take account of many social and economic problems. Nevertheless, when these problems are finally considered, with all their implications, we somehow sense that their solutions should not be allowed to 'lead to a contraction in the size of the national dividend'.

[1] As reported in *The Times*, 21 October, 1954.